The New Age Millionaires

Moshe R. Shokane

To my wife Susan, my wonderful son Tsebo, my two daughters Dimpho and Pearl.

To my mentor Manny Asada and my business partners Hajah Fauzia and Dr. Majola

To the entire family of Aim Global.

Copyright © 2018 by MR.SHOKANE

All rights reserved. No part of this publication may be reproduced, distributed, or transmitted in any form or by any means, including photocopying, recording, or other electronic or mechanical methods, without the prior written permission of the publisher, except in the case of brief quotations embodied in critical reviews and certain other non-commercial uses permitted by copyright law. For permission requests, write to the publisher, addressed "Attention: Permissions Coordinator," at the address below.

Johannesburg, Benoni 1515, South Africa Ordering Information: Quantity sales. Special discounts are available on quantity purchases by corporations, associations, and others. For details, contact the publisher at the address above.

Orders : r.shokane@gmail.com

ISBN-13:978-1720605652

Dean Alfange

I do not choose to be a common man.

It is my right to be uncommon … if I can.

I seek opportunity … not security.

I do not wish to be a kept citizen,

Humbled and dulled by having the State look after me.

I want to take the calculated risk,

To dream and to build. To fail and to succeed.

I refuse to barter incentive for a dole

I prefer the challenges of life to the guaranteed existence;

The thrill of fulfilment to the stale calm of Utopia.

I will not trade freedom for beneficence

Nor my dignity for a handout

I will never cower before any master

Nor bend to any threat.

It is my heritage to stand erect, proud and unafraid;

To think and act for myself,

To enjoy the benefit of my creations

And to face the world boldly and say:

This, with God's help, I have done.

All this is what it means to be an Entrepreneur

Contents

Why The New Age Millionaires 8
Learn, unlearn and relearn 17
How do you become free from the ego 27
Getting a job should be temporary 36
Believe that you will succeed 43
How to deal with fear 54
Your attitude determines your altitude ….. ………   69
How to use your story to win prospect ………….   78
Invest in yourself and reinvest in your business …   101
What I learned from Robert Kiyosaki ………   104
How to choose a network marketing company and why I chose Aim Global………………   118
Keeping your integrity in network marketing…   136
Upline and downline relationship…………….   141
Why giving is important? / Alive foundation………   144
How to think big   150

"In a time of drastic change, it is the learners who inherit the future. The learned usually find themselves equipped to live in a world that no longer exists."

— Eric Hoffer, Reflections on the Human Condition

Why The New Age Millionaires?

Achieving success on a high level has been for many people for a long time an unfulfilled dream. Many people just didn't believe in the fact they could accomplish something similar like what Steve Jobs did with Apple or what Bill Gates did with Microsoft. They believed that only the 'special' amongst us could achieve the extraordinary. However, in today's world that's no longer a justifiable excuse. People often say that the world we live in today has so much more opportunities to offer to people who want to succeed. I was always intrigued by this finding. So, I decided to mark down what the big differences were between the pre-digital age and today's world. When I started to do this, I became really motivated and more confident in the possibility to achieve massive success.

Why The New Age Millionaires?

If you've got something really unique to offer to the world, but nobody knows about you and your service then you're setting yourself up for failure. A couple years ago you needed television, the radio or the newspapers to get your ideas in front of an audience. This was really an obstacle to most people, because many people couldn't afford to advertise on these expensive platforms. So only the big companies or the individuals who already accumulated a lot of wealth could afford a good marketing campaign. However, nowadays things have become much easier with regards to marketing. Social media has revolutionized everything, especially YouTube and Facebook. If it weren't for YouTube & Facebook many brands and individuals wouldn't be as successful as they are right now.

These brands and individuals used YouTube & Facebook to get their name 'out there' and to let everybody know what they had to offer to the world. Through this way, many brands became 7 figure businesses and many individuals also became high-earners. Now we have more social media platforms than only Facebook and YouTube. A few other big platforms are Instagram, LinkedIn and Pinterest. The best part of it all is that these platforms allow you to market your services/product for free to a targeted audience, since people only follow you if they're interested in what you have to offer. So, it's no longer required to pay for presenting your services or products to an audience. All these platforms have something unique to offer, so find the one that suits you or your company the best and start showing the world what you have to offer.

A big complaint in the pre-digital period was the difficult access to the right information. Sure, there were seminars and books. And yes, there were also mentors available during the pre-digital period. However, not everybody could afford it to go to seminars and not everybody could connect that easily with mentors. These obstacles to access critical knowledge for their ideas discouraged many entrepreneurs which ultimately made them quit on their goals, because they didn't believe that they would ever get access to the right resources. Fortunately, in today's world that's no longer the case. All thanks to the World Wide Web. There are so many ways to learn from the internet and this all happens just by sitting behind your 'screen'. You can watch video clips, webinars, interviews, listen to seminar recordings or just read books. You can find almost anything that you want on the internet if you know what you're looking for.

The internet can help you so much with your business, because you can use it as a frame of reference. For example, if you aren't sure about something, you can just look it up. Or when you want to know what your competitors are doing then you can also just look it up. The access to all these types of knowledge increases the chance that you're staying on track on the road to success and that you aren't making mistakes that could have been easily avoided.

Ever since I heard about the concept of network marketing. I couldn't stop thinking about the endless opportunities it provides. In the process, I became a leader and a speaker. I discovered my true potential and I believed that this is an ongoing process. In the process, I met extraordinary human beings with frightening ambitions. I read financial and inspirational books. I found myself listening to tapes and digging deep in the mind of the successful. As my mentor would say that 'true education begins after school' I believe that life is the best teacher. In this book I will also share the most important lessons I have learned in life. As a young boy growing in the poor part of South Africa, I was clueless about network marketing. The narrative for me was to find a job and buy a house for my single mother who raised us under hardships. So, I went to school and I studied hard to become a teacher. I travelled the world teaching English. Now that I have bought my mom a house, the question is what's next? Was this all I wanted to achieve? The answer is no. I am still alive, Cleary there's more. I wanted to be part of the bigger picture. I wanted to give more to the world and contribute to the charity organisations of my choice. People remember your contributions to the world than the assets you have attained for yourself. I wanted to leave a legacy

 As a teacher, I noticed that the education we give to the students doesn't help them much in real life. I noticed that most of my friend are running the rat race. Their success depends on promotion at the workplace. I then remember a conversation I had with a gentleman from London who holds a PhD. He kept talking about CV's and finding another good paying job. ' A job! That was his notion of success. Most people are satisfied with where they are in life. They are happy with just doing enough to get by. I wanted more, I knew there was more, only if I stretch my potential and be willing to go all out for my dreams.

A lot of people join network marketing primordially to make money and that for them is success. They view success as the finish line. For an athlete, success is crossing the finish line. For me, crossing the finish line is part of it, there are crucial factors that one should take note of before starting the race. They should take into consideration that it takes persistence and strong desire to succeed. Before the race, warming up is important, the right attire, the right mindset, knowing that at some point their body and mind will want to give up, and what's going to keep them on the track. The healthy diet is also important. Without taking these factors into consideration, your chances of succeeding are rather slim or non-existent at all. This is another reason why I wrote this book. To give people the right tools they need to run the race of network marketing. To have the right approach to this thing called life. The competition in this business is with no one, but yourself. We always race to be better than we were yesterday. The willingness to persist despite obstacles.

I will also talk about company that is close to my heart. A company that has turned my life around. I am going to show you how to succeed in network marketing, particularly in Aim Global. The knowledge in this book will help you to manage your team and nurture it to grow. This book will share successful stories of networkers and their testimonials.

Aim Global has created more millionaires in a short period of time. This is simply done by distributing world class unique health products all over the globe. The concept of leverage has become a reality to me, because of Alliance in Motion global, I managed to do more with less.

My deepest gratitude goes first and foremost to Dr. Eduardo Cabantog, Mr. Raymond Asperin and Engr. Francis Miguel. The entire family of Aim Global for making this a reality. With the help of other distributors online, we managed to compile brief background of directors: Dr. Eduardo Cabantog is a graduate of Medicine from Pamantasan Lungsodng Maynila, a pioneer, leader, and model institution of higher learning in the Philippines. After acquiring his license as a Medical Doctor and serving as a company physician in one of the well-known local medical and clinical services provider for a couple of years. He practiced his medical expertise in some of the most reputable hospitals in the Philippines. He ventured into the networking business and joined other networking companies before instituting Alliance in Motion Global, Inc. in 2006. His remarkable success in his newly found career and having survived difficult challenges moulded a great leader and survivor fit to lead a fast-growing company in a world of multi-level marketing business where the competition is very stiff. Mr. Asperin was a graduating student when he started to venture into networking business because of his being adventurous and a young adult full of ambition and determination. He never lets a single opportunity slip away from his hands. He also believes that the future depends on the decisions we make today because life is not a matter of "chance", but it is a matter of "choice". He is known as "Mr. Excitement" because of his jolly spirit and inventiveness in promoting the company and its products. His creativity and effective ideas are the characteristics that make him unique in many ways. Mr. Asperin is indeed an achiever in the networking business and he travels around the country to share his history of success to better equip our distributors in pursuing their networking career. A Bachelor of Science in Computer Engineering graduate of Adamson University. He was hired by the leading telecommunications company in the Philippines right after graduating in college. He earned respect in the industry after creating millionaires that have become icons in the world of multi-level marketing business. He is one of the pioneer networker that has mentored some of the famous personalities in the industry. He is fondly called as the "mentor of all mentors". He has made alliance with all these icons and together they established a fast-growing networking company in the Philippines today, the Alliance In Motion Global, Inc.

Learn, relearn and unlearn

It was Alvin Toffler who wrote: the illiterate of the 21st century will not be those who cannot read and write, but those who cannot learn, unlearn, and relearn. "throughout my journey as an expatriate, I have met different types of people from all over the globe. I noticed one common factor that all these people possess. The willingness to learn and explore the world. The desire to discover more than they have already discovered. Their passion for education is unrelenting. For me to achieve what I have achieved thus far I had to unlearn and relearn. My teachers always told me that saving money was important, having a life policy that would take care of my family once I'm gone was the best financial decision I could ever have made. That letting someone else control my finances, while I go to work was the right thing to do. These are some behavioural patterns that we learn unconsciously. My father tried to do networking and he failed and that became part of him. It became a wall that he couldn't move for many years. Our education system punishes students for failing a test. Failure is viewed in isolation to success, whereas, failing is the crucial part of success. Our education system is designed like a fairy-tale with happy ending. It does less or nothing to prepare students for the real life.

Harrison Barnes on the importance of unlearning said that: *We perceive life as being constantly in motion and in a forward state of progress. Harrison Barnes further contents that:* Further, as humans, we are all designed for growth and for movement. As long as each of us is growing and progressing, we experience a sense of satisfaction and a sense of meaning or purpose in our lives. Once we stop growing, we start feeling a sense of *stagnation* and our lives become much less satisfying to us. In nature, when something stops moving, it's typically getting ready to die. I unequivocally believe if one hasn't found the purpose for living, he will find something to fill up the empty space, some fill up the space with alcohol and spirits, some with drugs so that they could escape from reality. Barnes believe that in order to experience success in our lives, we must focus on personal growth, as an incredibly important *activity*, and a process that bears many rewards. The sort of growth I have in mind, however, is different from what many people may instinctively think upon hearing the word 'growth'. When most of us think about growing, we think about perhaps reading more books to help us improve, meeting new people, and taking up new hobbies. There are, of course, many forms of growth, most of which involve learning. We have a sense that if we're *learning* more, we're growing.

However, I believe one of the most important forms of growth we can undertake is *unlearning*. All the learning we do, in a sense, involves unlearning. The more we can *unlearn*, the more likely we are to experience the sense of growth and progress we so desire. Mostly unlearning means letting go of false beliefs and assumptions that we've formerly used to govern our existence. *Letting go is unlearning.* For example, you may believe someone else is responsible for your own unhappiness; therefore, you believe this other person must change. Oftentimes when we are unhappy, we become obsessed with changing another individual who we believe is responsible for our condition. At some point, through learning, we may discover we're suffering due to our beliefs or our perceptions about the other person. For example, if you see someone at the mall, you may have an image of him or her that relates to someone you imagine doesn't like you. If you choose to hold this image, you will experience insecurity. Similarly, you may choose to *let go* of this image and *unlearn* it. When you unlearn a feeling of insecurity or anger, you will no longer have that negative reaction each time you see that person. That person actually hasn't changed—only your perception of him or her has.

As you grow by *unlearning*, you flower into joy. When you're joyful, you're a much happier person. Imagine how much more productive your life would be if you could unlearn many of the beliefs and behaviours that have caused you so much stress. You and your life would be utterly and completely transformed. This would result in an incredible *sea change* in the way you approach and live your life. In fact, if you can make a concerted effort to *unlearn*, your life will probably undergo a dramatic and welcome change.

My newfound ability and *choice* to unlearn various behaviours and beliefs has made a notable difference in my quality of life. Largely, I've been able to eliminate the "charge" and sense of discomfort I feel with various people, places, and things. Instead of putting my energy into feeling uncomfortable, I can now put my energy into feeling good and into more productive pursuits.

Your life is going to change when you learn how to channel energy that was formerly being consumed with unproductive anger and tension, into something productive. Nowhere will this change be as effective as when you apply it to your job search and career.

In our job searches and careers, most of us are continually feeling one tension after another. We have all sorts of defensive behaviours we've learned. In many cases, we spend more time *protecting an image of ourselves* than we do simply *being*. In so doing we waste a ton of energy on being defensive and staking various positions. This can harm us and keep us from achieving our goals.

Several years ago, I had an employee in Vereeniging. She started working for us at minimum wage. Because our company was so busy, within a few weeks of our hiring this person, she was given an increasing level of responsibility. And within a few months, she was earning over R54k a month working for one of our student loan companies. I didn't know this girl's age at the time, all I knew was that she was a model of hard work, productivity, and dedication. Interestingly enough, from what I recall, this employee didn't even have a high school diploma.

A friend of mine happens to be an internationally famous consultant and best-selling author who spends a good portion of his time consulting with companies about how to hire. He once came to visit me and spent time with me in our offices. After meeting over 100 of our employees, and observing several of them over a course of a few days, he knew very little about what this particular young woman did. One evening, a couple of weeks later, I was speaking with him on the phone and he said something to me I will never forget:

"The best person in your company is that 19-year-old girl. She is absolutely incredible," he told me.

"What are you talking about?" I asked. I couldn't believe this. At the time, I had graduates of the best law schools and colleges in South Africa working for the company. Moreover, this girl could barely put together a proper sentence. Also, work ethic aside, her temperament was quite out of control. A week or so earlier, she had gotten kicked out of a restaurant where we were all having dinner–for getting drunk and lighting up a cigarette in the middle of the restaurant. Smoking is a big "no no" in restaurants in Johannesburg. To my astonishment, this girl also fought with the people in the restaurant after she was kicked out. I didn't interfere with the young woman's behaviour, and have admittedly never run such a "tight ship" as to reprimand her for the incident, but I must admit the event was notable.

"She doesn't care what people think. She's like steel. Everyone out there is *posturing* and this holds them back. This girl says and does what she feels. She will be unstoppable in sales. I would hire her in a second from you. She has the exact same temperament I look for and spend months trying to find sales for the companies I consult for. She is the rarest but absolute best sort of person to get working for you."

I didn't think much about it at the time; however, in pondering this girl's remarkable success later in life, I'm confident that this apparent tenacity was the secret to her incredible success. Basically, she felt no fear in situations where most others surely would. Fearing something is a response or behaviour that many of us should analyse more deeply in ourselves and in some cases, unlearn because it can keep us from moving forward towards our goals.

Most people are "positioners." In any given conversation you have, you will likely take a "position" and the person with whom you're conversing will also take a position. Unlearning "positioning" is something that can make a drastic difference in your career and life, as this position is usually related to how you feel about yourself and how you expect others to feel about you as well. It's as if you have an identity that you're striving to defend in some way. Once you take a position, all you care about is defending it to prove you're right. This belief comes from the Ego Self, which can be characterized as follows:

Statements or beliefs such as "I'm right, you're wrong"

Dominating others

Making others feel guilty

Covering up facts

Never admitting the truth

Giving constant justification to others for your opinions

When the ego becomes too forceful, learning ceases. It becomes more important to be *right* than to learn.

To succeed in network marketing, you need to be a lifelong learner.' We have heard this saying a lot, and it's true. Learning makes us better people. While learning new things is great, some of this acquired knowledge might be counterproductive. That's when we need to "unlearn.

What to Unlearn

Unlearning is the art of discarding something that we learned earlier. To know what to unlearn, you need to be self-aware about your thoughts, beliefs, and your habits.

Examples of such thoughts and habits include, "Money is limited and scarce," "Luck plays a major role in success," Sacrificing health for success," etc.

You need to figure out the thoughts and habits that are holding you back and unlearn them.

Here's how I overcame the thought, "Money is limited and scarce." I used to have a feeling that money was limited before I came to know about entrepreneurship. This was because the people I was surrounded by were all working for someone, and they put that thought in my head at a very young age.

When I re-educated myself that money is something that can be earned when you can provide a quality service or product, it totally changed my perception about money. Now I offer my services to people who need them, and they pay me money. The more people I offer my services to, the more money I make. Simple!

How to Unlearn?

Here's a simple way to get started:
1. List any five thoughts and beliefs that are holding you back or are limiting your true potential.
2. List any five activities that aren't productive, but still, you keep doing them.
3. Re-educate yourself on those subjects, and take action for at least 21 days based on the *new* knowledge you've learned.

When you apply this to various parts of your life and take action on a consistent basis, you'll start seeing positive changes in your life. Learning is important, but unlearning is more important as it will give you a whole new perspective on the existing beliefs you have. Learn to empty your cup before filling it!

So what are those things that you want to unlearn?

_____
_____
_____
_____
_____

How do you become free from 'the' ego?

The best way is to pay attention to those around you. When people start relating to a label or classification, and you find them falling into the categories mentioned above, they are primarily using the ego to make decisions.

We like relating to our closest friends because they typically love and support us as we are. In contrast, the ego is a *perception* and not necessarily who someone really *is*. The ego is a sense of existence, and a game played by the mind. The mind wants a sense of certainty and security, and it seeks this security through the perception it creates.

In relationships, it often becomes important to win. Our winning becomes more important than our partner–or even ourselves, or our relationship. The ego is trying to rush you away. When we play ego games, we become concerned with things like "I'm right and you're wrong," and refusing to be dominated. We also use

How do you become free from the ego?

guilt in an attempt to dominate the other person. Ego games are fun to watch, but not always constructive for those at play.

For many people, every time there's a conversation they want to prove they're right. If you can't feel right, you then may try and make the other person feel guilty. Why does the ego play all of these games? Simply to survive. The need to become someone is why we try and prove we're right all of the time. When the ego is involved people become positional.

However, the ego makes us self-centered, which often leads to a failure of intelligence. Instead of doing things for the correct reasons, you may do something just to prove you're right, and you will do this even if you know the decision you're making may mean a loss to you, for example, a financial loss. All for simply trying to prove you're right.

What does the ego need for itself?

The ego is constantly becoming. By trying to become free of the ego, you can never lose it. However, when you become aware of the ego, it can no longer make use of you. In trying to become free of the ego, you end up strengthening it. Awareness of the ego gives you the choice to dominate or not dominate using the ego. You may choose to become positional in a conversation or not. All learning is unlearning. I'm focusing on unlearning the various assumptions that cause suffering. Often, we think we're being truthful, but being truthful isn't necessarily authentic. Being authentic helps us move forward and embrace who we are. The greatest threat to our happiness and lives is failing to properly integrate our own inadequacies. Instead of dealing with our own inadequacies, we try and overthrow others. This may seem like an easier solution, but in reality, it's not. Being authentic means being able to confront our own shortcomings. When we embrace our shortcomings, something beautiful happens. Embracing *the real issue* gives us freedom.

"In a time of drastic change, it is the learners who inherit the future. The learned find themselves equipped to live in a world that no longer exists" Eric Hoffer

In an article posted By Patricia Young on 08/30/2016 she postulates that: Part of being an entrepreneur (a networker) is having to face failure, and learning from our mistakes, so we can learn something new and course-correct when needed. But, if we

How do you become free from the ego?

are afraid of failing, most of the times, we will hold ourselves back and will not even try to take different risks or do things in a different way, which could help us grow ourselves and our business.

Becoming a networker requires a whole new mindset. We need to unlearn so many things that we've been taught. And unlearning can take work, because it requires that we get awareness of the habits, beliefs and behaviours that have been driving our lives, on auto-pilot, for years. Unlearning requires that we confront an uncomfortable reality, so we can allow ourselves to grow and move closer to our goals as heart-cantered entrepreneurs.

At the end of the day, how can we grow and see different results in our life and business, if we're not willing to see the truth, and if we continue doing the same things, and making the same kind of choices, over and over again, right?

I believe that giving ourselves permission to explore, from a place of curiosity, and having the willingness to change whatever needs to change, so we can honour and fulfil our mission here on the planet, is one of the most beautiful acts of self-love. In order to unlearn habits and beliefs we need to make the conscious choice, have the willingness to be open and be mindful of what shows up for us. Here are 2 additional important tips:

How do you become free from the ego?

. Be curious – reconnect with your inner-child and keep asking ourselves questions like: "why", "how can I" and "what if". That way we'll be able to be more creative about finding solutions, at a much different level and with a different mindset.

Connect with other people that have what you want – find people who can give you a different perspective, which will open your mind to other possibilities and will push you in a new direction. Here are some of the things that you'll need to unlearn if you want to become a networker:

Waiting for someone to tell you what to do – you're your own boss, therefore, you're the one that will be determining your strategies, managing your time and creating some type of structure during the day so you can stay focused and accomplish your goals. This was a big one for me, and I've seen that this is a common struggle for many other entrepreneurs that are just starting a business, after many years of working for corporate.

Avoiding Failure – The only failure is not trying… The surest way to *not* succeed is by not trying to do things differently, not showing up, not stepping up, not putting yourself out there. Failure is not a reason to feel shame at all. Failure is part of the process of becoming successful, because we learn with every experience. Failing and making mistakes brings growth, and you can always course-correct.

Blaming others and circumstances – We always have to take responsibility for the results we get in life and business. When you blame others or your circumstances you are giving your power away and are seeing yourself as a victim. Just know that you have the power to be, do, and have whatever you want. As networker, you're responsible for the results you create in your business. It's all about your mindset.

Leaning towards perfectionism – It's ok to try to get things done in a professional way, but don't fall into the trap of perfectionism. Fear is behind perfectionism, so don't wait for all the stars to align or having everything figured out before you start your business or launch a new product/service. Just do it, and then you can always tweak things. Just think about some companies, like Microsoft windows, their software has different versions. That means that they have been improving along the way.

Being an employee, you need to just do your thing – Being an networker takes more than just one job. It takes many jobs to make up a business! You have to wear many different hats to run your business, so you need to learn the business of doing business. An employee will get paid for being busy, but a networker gets paid for results. You are responsible for the bottom line, and believe me, busy-ness without a focus and a plan, will not pay your bills.

Being weak when setting boundaries – You need to learn to create better and healthier boundaries. Saying "No" with kindness to others, will mean saying "yes" to yourself and your business. Setting clear boundaries is a key leadership skill that you need in order to succeed, and take your business dreams seriously.

Not communicating your truth – Holding yourself back from being authentic and vulnerable, will not only hold your business growth, but will also create weak and superficial relationships. It takes courage to be more assertive and speak your truth, but doing so will create connection with others and will attract ideal clients that are needing your gifts. Like Brene Brown says: "Owning your story can be hard, but not nearly as difficult as spending our lives running from it." I truly believe that courage always creates a ripple effect because, every time we choose courage, we inspire others to do the same. Like with everything else, allowing yourself to be courageous and honouring your truth, is a matter of choice.

Being unaware of your attitude – Attitude is key to success. You have to become aware and be mindful of your attitude and your

How do you become free from the ego?

thinking. Choosing to stay positive, despite the challenges that you'll face, will make a big difference. Also, when you're faced with rejections from potential clients, because you will, don't make it about you, don't take it personal. Just keep going and stay focused on your next steps to achieve your goals.

Looking for answers and happiness outside of yourself – the power is always inside of you. Create a ritual in which you connect with your centre every day, so you can stay grounded and positive. Doing this, will help you feel more confident, make better decisions and will allow you to stay committed to your goals, regardless of the setbacks that you will be facing as an entrepreneur. Your well-being and peace don't depend on external factors, this will only act as a quick fix that is not sustainable.

One more thing, find a mentor! I've had many mentors along the way. I've been paying for coaches myself, because I know that I need support and it will make the process and learning curve easier for me. I also follow other mentors, read their books, sign up for a few online courses, go to workshops, etc.

I know that I get better results as I surround myself with like-minded people who will inspire me and see the greatness in me, even when I can't see it sometimes. That is part of my commitment and how I stay faithful to the amazing process of

How do you become free from the ego?

being an entrepreneur, so I share my gifts with the world. And I want you to do the same, because I know, with 100% certainty, that your gifts are needed. *Patricia Young* is one the gifted thinkers in our lifetime. She inspired me to think big and unleash the power within me. My deepest gratitude to her and may she continue to touch more lives.

Getting a job should be temporary

There must be more to success than just getting a job, or millions of people around the world would be a lot more successful than they are. If you are at work right now, think about the investment of time and energy you are making. Imagine that you only went home to sleep for four hours a night, and gave up all the rest of your personal time to get more work done. Imagine that you practically lived at your desk and worked your tail off for the next five years. What would that extraordinary effort get you?

If you're working for a fixed salary or hourly wage the way most people are, you won't see economic benefits from pouring your energy into your job. Your boss may be grateful to you for all your extra effort, but he or she is not going to give you a pay raise every month just because you're putting in extra hours. You're not going to get paid more just because you have great ideas. None of those investments on your part translate into tangible career success. You could donate every working hour to your job and still get a one percent pay bump at the end of the year, or get laid

Getting a Job should be temporary.

off when the company realizes that you've solved all their biggest problems and they don't need you anymore.

We can see that there's more to career success than just hard work -- so what's the magic ingredient?

The magic ingredient to success is not the good fortune to come from a wealthy family, and it isn't a great education, either, as plenty of underemployed but highly-educated people can attest. The magic ingredient for career success and satisfaction is self-determination. When you are the captain of the ship, you get to decide which way to sail.

Les Brown (2015) postulates , Are you in a contract with mediocrity? Have you settled for what you get...not what you want? One of the best things that happened to me was getting fired from a job where they paid me just enough to keep me from quitting and I worked just enough to keep from getting fired. Sometimes when you do not have enough insight or courage to leave a situation that you have outgrown...life will move on you! Break the contract with being average and playing small. The penalty for keeping this in your life just is not worth it. You owe it to yourself to reach higher and to create something that is really you! You have something special. You have GREATNESS within you!!"

Getting a Job should be temporary.

Now that you know that your job is not the best solution

Here are the facts about network marketing.

Network Marketing has created more millionaires than any other business.

Network Marketing is the short-cut to financial freedom, they're aren't any short-cuts to the short-cut.

Network Marketing is NOT a Pyramid Scam, if it were; the government would have shut them all down long ago (yes, there are some scams out there, just do your homework).

Every typical corporation is a pyramid structure. You have a CEO or President at the top, under them are directors, under them are managers, under them are supervisors, who have a bunch of worker bees at the bottom doing all the work! So, who makes more?...the person at the top or the bottom...duh! Where do you want to be?

Network Marketing is simply word of mouth or referral marketing...period. You get paid for moving products, that's it.

Leverage...The Real Power of Network Marketing!

What is the maximum amount of time you could possibly work in a week? If you worked 6 days a week, 24 hours a day you would have 144 hours of productive work.

Getting a Job should be temporary.

Let's look at it a different way…if you had only 50 distributors in your organization all working part time for 8 hours a week you would have 400 hours of productivity going into your business every week.

That is 256 more hours than you could achieve working 6 days a week, 24 hours a day!

Does that seem fair? It is absolutely fair! This is what the wealthy know and implement!

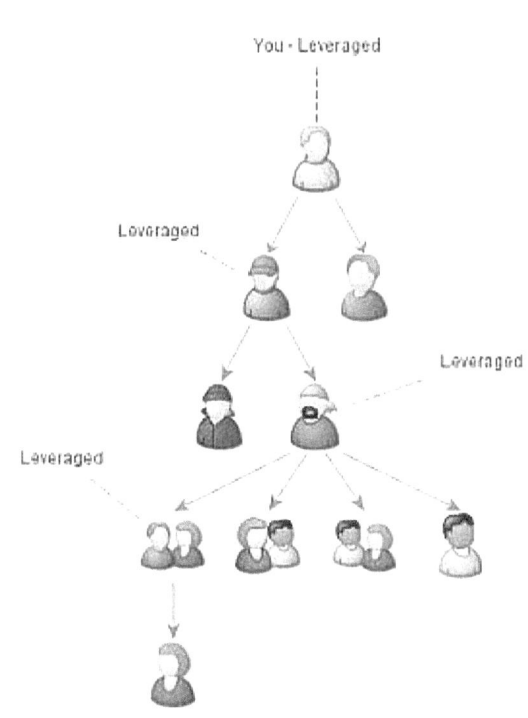

Freedom

Getting a Job should be temporary.

Live the lifestyle of a millionaire; without the burdens, hassles, and responsibilities.

Your time and your life are yours to spend as you wish, live the life you deserve.

Perpetual Residual Income Stream:

The income can be passed on to your family or heirs.

Better than a life insurance policy because the money keeps rolling in, month after month, year after year.

There is no limit to how much you can earn.

Be Your Own Boss:

Working for yourself…whether it be part time or full time is better than any J-O-B. Why, you ask…because most people drive 30 minutes or more to work…fighting traffic…to go to a job they don't like…to work with people they don't want to…to make someone else rich…only to get laid off at a moment's notice…and the weird part is…they're afraid of losing that…I don't get it…heck, I'd be glad to get fired… shall I continue…

Tax Advantages:

Legally put dollars in your pocket from having a home-based business. It's not what you make; it's what you can keep!

Even if your business doesn't make money at first, you're still ahead by having the tax write-offs.

Small Start-up Costs:

Getting a Job should be temporary.

Most Network Marketing businesses can be launched for $500 or less, some are free; try and start a franchise like McDonald's for that price.

Superior Products:

Most products are as good as or better than their retail counterparts.

NO Restrictions:

NO set hours

NO traffic / commute

NO employees

NO dress code

NO high overhead

NO limitations

NO office politics.

Open to All:

Regardless of your age, sex, race, education, experience, income level, capital investment, family or business background, past successes or failures; no restrictions of any kind…just roll up your sleeves and make it happen

Training / Support:

I can only succeed if you do…so it's in my best interest to make you as successful as possible, its win-win for all.

Getting a Job should be temporary.

Corporate America is just the opposite, do you think your boss is going to train you to take his job...I don't think so..

Take control of you...and own your life? Start Network Marketing!

Believe that you will succeed

People often say, "if I can see it, I will believe" this is a mindset of unsuccessful people. *Wayne Dyer* says that if you can believe it, you will see it.

The universe will not give you a challenge you can't handle. Triumph is already within us. The mere fact that we survived million sperms, clearly that should mean something. 'Whatever you want in life is already within you'. people always get confused when I say this. This might sound mundane and obvious, but many people do not believe that their dreams are necessarily. If you have been rejected before that might cause disbelief, hence it's important to adapt a growth mindset. Believe that if Nelson Mandela could do it, you can also do it. Realize that everything you see around you was created by humans who believed that it's possible. When we were kids we used to dream, but as we grow up we tend loose our focus. That's because of the habits we have unconsciously learned along the way. You have shift your mind to a space of believe. I think that is the most rewarding place to get to, the place where you as an individual has what it takes in order to succeed.

Belief that what you want is possible, belief in your own abilities, belief in the systems that you need to put in place to get there. Believe in the product you are distributing. One gentleman told me that believe is contagious, therefore it's easy to see the difference between a salesman whose goal is make money and the one whose goal is to satisfy the customer.

In order to succeed or reach a goal, we must believe in ourselves that we will reach our goals. Dale Carnegie once said, "Believe that you will succeed – and you will." The way we see ourselves and how we think of ourselves can create a huge impact on what we do. And when you are on the path to success, some people will tear you down. But if we strongly believe in our success, then all those discouraging words will not affect us. Success doesn't come easy, that's a known fact. It is about hard work and dedication. But it also requires strong determination. With that determination is the belief in succeeding. Successful entrepreneurs knew from day one that they would succeed, no matter how tough and rough things will go. They believed in their success even before they made it happen; and that belief helped them through it.

Believe that you will succeed

You are the main agent to your success. Your goals will depend on you for life. If you treat them like they mean nothing to, they will forever remain nothing to you. However, if you treat them like your life depends on them, they will give you reasons to live fully and die fulfilled. You have to decide right now that you are going to take your goals seriously. You are going stop waiting for success and rather go get success. Don't worry about the difficulties and challenges that you will encounter. They are nothing but stepping stones. Your creator will not put you through any test he has not prepared you for.

Embrace challenges with believe and conviction. With your eyes gazing at your goals, you will survive all forms of storms and reach your greatness. You are chosen for greatness! You are truly born to win! Stay motivated

Whenever we board on a plane, we believe that we will get to our destination. A single doubt will make one not to board on the plane. Hence once you choose Aim Global, it's important to have 100% belief in the company and its products. Most of the people join network marketing primarily for money. However, I think it's important to know that money is not with the company you have joined but the people you will serve. Once the people are satisfied with the products and service, money would not be a problem. I believe one should join network marking for a much bigger dream than just money. When I started recruiting medical doctors into my network I strongly believed that the products do work. The doctors then recommended the products to their patients and I can't tell you how many times people have called me to thank me. This brings satisfaction to me of course

Believers are pioneers and pioneers are believers. Pioneers have courage to start even though there's nothing tangible to prove that whatever they are doing will succeed. John F Kennedy announced that American astronauts will fly to the moon. At the time of the announcement America didn't have enough resources to fly to the moon.

In 2016 when I heard about Aim Global, I flew to Kenya from south Africa to listen to the presentation. I couldn't sleep the night after the presentation, because of the size of the dream I had. I then started my group in south Africa without the branch. What this meant was we had to order products from Manila. Some of our products got confiscated at the customs and we lost lots of money that didn't belong to us. We had to come up with a plan to repay the members. Most of them quit because of the incident, but we kept on moving because we had faith in the company.

We knew that to register any type of medicine in South Africa takes about 3 years or more to be approved. Time was not a problem. We knew that we were pioneers and because we had faith and belief in the company we kept moving. Confucius "it does not matter how slowly you go as long as you do not stop" Harriet Beecher Stowe " when you get into a tight place and everything goes against you, till it seems as though you could not hold on a minute longer, never give up then, for that is just the place and time that the tide will turn"

Be patient! Give your dream time. Don't abandon your dream because of the time it'll take to start giving you success. Set your eyes on the goals and not the time it will take. Many people have given up on their dreams because of the time it takes to start achieving success. They are not patient. They have failed to know that it takes time for important and valuable dream to bring great success. Resolve to keep pursuing your dream passionately. Decide to keep sharpening your skills and waiting for opportunity to come at the appropriate time. The time you're most prepared to showcase your talent to the world with hunger for success. Know that you can only be hopeful on what you've started and not what you are visualising. People that give excuses about pursuing their dreams because of the time it'll take to start giving back are the ones that end up not doing anything at all. Take a step toward success now and don't worry about the time it'll take to achieve it.

Les Brown " live full, die empty" is a motif that weaves itself through Maya Angelou's books, and is realized at the conclusion of *I Know Why the Caged Bird Sings*, when she is at last bonded with her mother, and about to become a mother herself. The notion that the individual possesses the power to live a fully realized life—despite barriers like race and gender and poverty—is woven throughout Angelou's work, and continues to inspire her legions of fans. A verse from her poem, "A Brave and Startling Truth," underscores this idea:

When we come to it We must confess that we are the possible... We are the miraculous, the true wonders of this world Free to choose our ends, and our new beginnings That is when, and only when... We come to it

Maya Angelou, may her soul rest in peace. She's the voice that spoke to me daily and this is what she said that inspired me to move forward.

"Life is not measured by the number of breaths we take, but by the moments that take our breath away."

"I've learned that people will forget what you said, people will forget what you did, but people will never forget how you made them feel."

"A bird doesn't sing because it has an answer; it sings because it has a song."

"I've learned that you can tell a lot about a person by the way he/she handles these three things: a rainy day, lost luggage and tangled Christmas tree lights."

"The first time someone shows you who they are, believe them."

"I can be changed by what happens to me. But I refuse to be reduced by it."

"Success is liking yourself, liking what you do and liking how you do it."

"You can only become truly accomplished at something you love. Don't make money your goal. Instead pursue the things you love doing and then do them so well that people can't take their eyes off you."

"Courage: the most important of all the virtues because without courage, you can't practice any other virtue consistently."

"If I am not good to myself, how can I expect anyone else to be good to me?"

"You alone are enough. You have nothing to prove to anybody."

"Surviving is important. Thriving is elegant."

"Nothing can dim the light which shines from within."

Have you ever heard a successful person talking about how achieving success went smooth without any obstacle to overcome or sacrifices to make? You don't, because there are none. Also, have you ever talked about success with just a random person, who didn't achieve something huge, but just lives an ordinary life like 99% of the people do? You probably have, and they probably were emphasizing how much effort and time you have to invest to become successful.

The difference between these two types of people should tell you enough. Your dream lifestyle doesn't exist yet, however we're fortunate enough that we're able to manifest that lifestyle by putting in the work and time. Many people have been in your shoes and those same people worked hard and smart to achieve their goals and dreams. So, listen to the advice of your friends, but take the advice from the successful people if you want to become one yourself.

The one thing you should worry about when you're in doubt about pursuing your dreams or staying in your comfort zone is the matter of time. The longer you stay indecisive the more valuable time you lose that you could have otherwise spent so much better.

Believe that you will succeed

You shouldn't feel rushed by time, because most likely you won't achieve the success you desire overnight. However, at the same time you should feel some sense of urgency, because the sooner you start working towards your goals, the faster you'll get to the place you want to be.

There are two types of people when approaching business: one just meets the requirements and the other one wants to excel at what he/she does. Be the latter one, because the first one is the attitude of mediocre people. They want to do everything in life with as little effort as possible. That's why these people never achieved the life they really wanted for themselves.

When you go all out on what you do, then not only will the results be much better, but you'll also leave a good impression on other people. When you consistently over-deliver, people start to acknowledge your achievements and want to get in contact with you, because who wouldn't want to work with someone who gives his 110% effort in everything?

You should not dismiss the advice that you get from people who you know have your best interest at heart. However, at the end of the day you should be the one that's in control of the decisions that you make in your life. For example, if you always dreamed about having your own multi-million-rand business that employs more than 100 people then who has the right to stop you?

Or maybe you always wanted to have your own restaurant in the town where you grew up. The choice is yours. You are the person who has to deal with the regret, in 10 years from now, if you decide not to pursue your dreams. The people who tell you that you shouldn't go after your dreams will be fine either way.

Going all in on your vision doesn't mean that you have to drop everything and focus on only what you want. Instead, it means that you should prioritize what makes you feel happy and fulfilled, because at the end of the day you are your longest commitment. Every person has something unique to offer to the world so don't let your dream be just a dream.

Believe that you will succeed

How to deal with fear

Everyone has gifts and talents that largely go unexplored and uncultivated. Fear is a powerful emotional that paralyze us and keeps us from achieving our goals and dreams. My writing is inspired by music and poetry. Allow yourself to read the following poem with understanding and imagine that you are reading it for the first.

Our Greatest Fear
Our greatest fear is not that we are inadequate,
but that we are powerful beyond measure.
It is our light, not our darkness, that frightens us.
We ask ourselves, Who am I to be brilliant,
gorgeous, handsome, talented and fabulous?
Actually, who are you not to be?
You are a child of God.

Your playing small does not serve the world.
There is nothing enlightened about shrinking

How to deal with fear

so that other people won't feel insecure around you.

We were born to make manifest the glory of God within us.
It is not just in some; it is in everyone.

And, as we let our own light shine, we consciously give
other people permission to do the same.
As we are liberated from our fear,
our presence automatically liberates others.

Author: Marianne Williamson

Bob Marley: Redemption songs

Old pirates, yes, they rob I
Sold I to the merchant ships
Minutes after they took I
From the bottomless pit
But my hand was made strong
By the hand of the Almighty
We forward in this generation
Triumphantly

How to deal with fear

Won't you help to sing

These songs of freedom?

'Cause all I ever have

Redemption songs

Redemption songs

Emancipate yourselves from mental slavery

None but ourselves can free our minds

Have no fear for atomic energy

'Cause none of them can stop the time

How long shall they kill our prophets

While we stand aside and look? Ooh

Some say it's just a part of it

We've got to fulfill the Book

Won't you help to sing

These songs of freedom?

'Cause all I ever have

Redemption songs

Redemption songs

Redemption songs

Emancipate yourselves from mental slavery

None but ourselves can free our minds

Wo! Have no fear for atomic energy

How to deal with fear

'Cause none of them-a can-a stop-a the time

How long shall they kill our prophets

While we stand aside and look?

Yes, some say it's just a part of it

We've got to fulfill the book

Won't you have to sing

These songs of freedom?

'Cause all I ever had

Redemption songs

All I ever had

Redemption songs

These songs of freedom

Songs of freedom

We no longer live in the age of slavery, except the chains we tie ourselves with. During the struggle of apartheid in South Africa, only the brave stood up and fought against the evil regime. While the cowards stood and watched. Fear kills dreams. One man once said that people die at the age of 30 but they are not buried till they are 60. Once you stop dreaming, you stop living. In the 21st century, no excuse is acceptable for failing. Technology and easy access to information makes us better than the people in the 19th

century. If people in the 19th century could do it, I'm adamant that you can do it better.

One of the biggest things for me was the day I realized that knowledge alone was not enough. You can know what you need to do without doing it. I think that's when you hit the level of true mediocrity- when you have the wisdom without the action. That's just a sign that fear controls you and keeps you from breaking free. To overcome this, you must have a "reason why" that's way more powerful than your fear. Find something that drives you and motivates you to the point where nothing can stand in your way!

Those who are living a truly fulfilling life are not necessarily those with big academic qualifications working in big companies but, those with big dreams; who are pursuing their dreams with unstoppable tenacity! I know a lot of people who quit their jobs at some prestigious companies to pursue their dreams. What is your dream? Find it. Chase it. Pursue it with everything at your command and take steps to work towards your dream to make it become a reality.

Today, change your thoughts change your life. Time for positive self-talk. Tell yourself:

"I can do anything I put my mind to. Whatever the circumstances I will get what I want and where I want to be. I can overcome any challenge. I can live the life of my dream".

Time to shift from negative thoughts to positive thoughts and to control your mind.

You can do this. Re-program your mind redirects your life. You have not seen the best of you yet.

I painstakingly chose the poem and the song meticulously for their meaning and relevance to the topic. We must break the shackles and free ourselves from the prison of shame and what other people may think? Be a good, compassionate and caring human being, live your life using the unmatched power of reason, common sense principles and ethical standards as your guide

We must never forget that morality, integrity, honour, honesty, ethics, reason and common sense are all combination of learned and built in human qualities and attributes. We should also understand that all of the criminal, violent conducts are all learned behaviour. We turn to focus our energy to what people will think of us doing the networking business. Well, what people think of you is not your business. Your business is what you think of yourself. We often get stuck in thinking what if I fail? What If I don't succeed. We become our own enemies and succumb to the fear of failure. I believe that people are generally scared of being rejected. Les brown once said that we should make no our vitamin. Whenever someone says no, we should know that we closer to a yes. The good thing about rejection is that it teaches us more about ourselves, we learn from our failures and improve ourselves to be better.

How can we overcome the fear of failure in network marketing? This is the question I get asked often as I meet a lot of new recruits. I believe one needs to invest in gaining knowledge about the company. Know who you are and why you joined network marketing industry. Mandela once said that it seems impossible until its done. Listening to motivational talks and reading books is one thing, but applying the knowledge that you have learned is another. Fear always puts us in our comfort zone. We rather do what's easy so that we don't fail and we are not willing to take risks. If we don't risk we won't grow, growth happens outside our comfort zone.

How to deal with fear

"Too many of us are not living our dreams because we are living our fears." ~Les Brown

Kari Dahlgren writes in her article titled: Fear used to be the driving force in my life.

I didn't even know that I was living in fear at the time. I hid behind labels like "stress" and "anxiety," but those are just clinical terms for fear.

Truthfully, my dreams terrified me because they seemed way too big to achieve. At the time, I wanted to excel in my new career, get into the best shape of my life, and create meaningful relationships—and I felt like I had a long way to go.

So naturally, I got really stressed out.

And why, oh why, did it feel okay?

It seems like stress is such commonplace now that we think we're slackers if we *don't* feel tense all the time. But that's just our fear finding excuses to stick around.

Once I finally realized that stress was just an option, I started looking for a way through it. And I found the answers in a simple Japanese philosophy called *Kaizen*, which is the practice of continuous improvement through small, consistent steps.

I learned that whenever we're scared about making change it's because the steps we're taking are too big, and these leaps of faith will trigger a life-saving biological response: fear.

But luckily, there's a way to turn that fear off, and it all starts with your brain, specifically your amygdala.

Eradicate Fear by Taking Small, Relentless Steps

Once you start asking tiny questions, then you can start taking tiny actions.

The key is to pick things that are small enough to keep your amygdala from getting in the way.

And that's why New Year's Resolutions never work. For example, on January 1st we decide that we want to lose twenty pounds and completely give up chocolate; so we restrict our calories and give up our vice all at the same time.

When you put yourself up against a mountain, the big steps you're forced to take will trigger your flight response and ultimately lead to stress and burnout.

If you want to achieve a big goal, you have to break it up into tiny steps.

I used this tiny-step tactic when I started focusing on becoming healthier. I didn't do anything radical—although that's how it started out, and I had to fail over and over until I realized radical wouldn't work.

Instead, I took the slow and steady route, and it was brutally slow. It took me about two years to really gain momentum, but it trained me to reject instant gratification and just go slow.

First, I started avoiding processed foods, and I focused on that until I mastered it. Then, I started focusing on only eating until I'm full, and I focused on that until I mastered it.

Then I started going to the gym two days a week and I kept it up until I gained the momentum I needed to go four days a week.

I didn't realize what I was doing at the time, but I proved to myself (and hopefully to you) that small steps are much more successful at making big change.

And I've become the healthiest version of myself because of it.

Get Excited—It's a Fearless Emotion

But what about the people who don't do tiny things? What about the people who do really big things and do them exceptionally well?

These people have a very special talent: They know how to get really excited about their goals, and excitement is another way to keep your flight response off.

So, if you want to successfully achieve your dreams, you need to get excited about them! It will help you avoid fear and take projects on with enthusiasm.

For example, my boss just gave me approval to write a book, which is something I've always wanted to do, and I was absolutely thrilled!

Instead of letting myself become overwhelmed by the size of this project, I chose to get over-the-moon excited about it, which helps me stay focused and creative.

Have you ever felt so fired up about an idea that you can't wait to start working on it? If so, don't ever let that feeling go. It will propel your dreams faster than anything.

But if you can't make the excitement last (and that's okay—fear likes to creep in any chance it gets), then try using visualization.

Train Your Brain with Visualization

To get yourself to do something that scares you, you need to visualize yourself doing it first. And you need to visualize it over and over because repetition is how your brain masters new skills. And if you consistently visualize it every day (and all you really need is just thirty seconds daily), you'll start to mentally master the action. Then all your body has to do is follow through.

The key to effective visualization is to involve excruciating detail.

You need to visualize what it's going to look like just as much as what it's going to *sound, feel, and emote like*. You also need to imagine how you'll react to different possible scenarios, including the worst possible outcome.

What will you do if you fail? What will the alternative actions be? How will you feel?

When you mentally train yourself to deal with potential failure, you won't give up when that bump in the road actually happens.

Apply These Concepts to Big and Small Goals

You can use visualization to accomplish anything and everything, even the super small stuff, which is where everyone should start. One of the best ways I've used visualization was to mentally train myself to say hello to strangers. It's such a small thing, but that's how I knew it could make a profound difference in my life. Saying hello to strangers was always something that I wanted to feel comfortable with, but I felt this unshakable resistance to it. And it all boiled down to being scared of rejection—something we people pleasers fear most.

Ah yes, I was terrified of how I would feel if people didn't say hello back. It's so silly and almost petty, but that's how my mind was programmed at the time.

So, I started visualizing myself doing this super simple task that I was afraid of. I would visualize myself saying hello to strangers in the supermarket while smiling and feeling whole (i.e. not seeking their approval).

I would also visualize the worst possible outcome, which is that they ignore me (so scary, I know), and I would visualize how I felt when that happened: still smiling and still whole.

Then I took this visualization into the real world.

I started smiling and saying hello to strangers, and I felt genuinely happy while doing it. Sometimes it would turn into engaging conversation, other times it would turn into absolutely nothing. But no matter what the outcome was, I was always smiling.

Using visualization this way helped me gain the momentum I needed to create meaningful relationships in my life. Today some of the most amazing people I know were once strangers that I simply said hello to.

Sometimes we resist small changes and small habits because they seem too easy to make a profound difference in our lives. But I challenge you to reject that notion.

But, the wonderful thing about failure is that it's entirely up to us to decide how to look at it.

We can choose to see failure as "the end of the world," or as proof of just how inadequate we are. Or, we can look at failure as the incredible learning experience that it often is. Every time we fail at something, we can choose to look for the lesson we're meant to learn. These lessons are very important; they're how we grow, and how we keep from making that same mistake again. Failures stop us only if we let them.

It's easy to find successful people who have experienced failure. For example:

Michael Jordan is widely considered to be one of the greatest basketball players of all time. And yet, he was cut from his high school basketball team because his coach didn't think he had enough skill.

Warren Buffet, one of the world's richest and most successful businessmen, was rejected by Harvard University.

Richard Branson, owner of the Virgin empire, is a high-school dropout.

Most of us will stumble and fall in life. Doors will get slammed in our faces, and we might make some bad decisions. But imagine if Michael Jordan had given up on his dream to play basketball when he was cut from that team. Imagine if Richard Branson had listened to the people who told him he'd never do anything worthwhile without a high-school diploma.

Think of the opportunities you'll miss if you let your failures stop you.

Failure can also teach us things about ourselves that we would never have learned otherwise. For instance, failure can help you discover how strong a person you are. Failing at something can help you discover your truest friends, or help you find unexpected motivation to succeed.

Often, valuable insights come only after a failure. Accepting and learning from those insights is key to succeeding in life.

Your attitude determines your altitude

Les Brown talks about spending your time with only quality people (OQP) he says that if you hang around with losers you will end up a loser. This is true, the people we spend time with influence our decisions in life.

There is nothing more exhilarating than being around people who exude the energy of endless possibilities. The OQP people are needed in our lives if we wish to see what is attainable. When we surround our environment with people who believe in the harshness of life we are drained of energy and vitality. Therefore, the choice is up to us - do we want to reach the stars or do we want to stay on the ground constantly looking up secretly wishing that we were among the dazzling jewels that grace the heavens. A strong, positive and resilient attitude will help elevate you to unimaginable heights.

In life attitude is everything. Check the people around you and observe their attitude barometer - negative or positive - and if the results are negative then you may need to look at your own attitude and make certain adjustments. Usually people mirror our own unconscious feelings and attitudes about life that we perhaps are not acknowledging head on. Remember, your attitude determines your altitude. That's why it's so important to be choosy about who we do spend our time with. I believe that we do become what we think about, and who we surround ourselves with every day strongly influences what we think about or become. A positive attitude is not about displaying a phony smile, a happy face and a perky disposition. It is simply a way of responding to life in a manner that allows us to accept the duality, the contradictions, the contrasts of our experiences. A positive attitude enables you to make a difference in the world around you because when you are able to see things in a positive light, you help to influence and shape other people's attitude as well. What is attitude anyway? It is the mental state or position you take regarding your life and affairs. This means it's not what you think but how you think it. Your attitude forms every event in your life, whether you realize it or not. Out of your attitude comes your enjoyment of life and gratitude for all your blessings. Out of your attitude also comes your disappointment and anger at how things have turned out. Out of attitude also comes the feeling that no accomplishment will be ever be good enough or that you are not

good enough. Everyday, your attitude is challenged by other people and by external factors. How will you react? Will you allow adversity to stop you from moving forward? Will you allow a negative person to ruin your day, make you lose your cool, or force you to give up on your dreams? When such temptations come knocking on your door, stand at the door of your mind and declare powerfully and silently, "No one is home". In other words, cease to engage.

At certain junctures in our lives, we will encounter challenging circumstances or people. We can either regard our dilemmas with anger, bitterness or frustration. Or we can look deep within and find the source that is beyond all circumstances and then pick ourselves up, dust ourselves off and move forward knowing all things will work in our favour. If on any given day, negative drama surrounds you, hang on to your own positive attitude and don't let other people to drag you down. Keep the words of George Washington in mind "Associate yourself with men of good quality if you esteem your own reputation, for 'tis better to be alone than be in bad company.'

We should stay away from the attitude of instant gratification. A lot of people join network marketing with the aim making quick money. They tend to quit if things don't happen time and quickly move to the next. These kinds of people have been hooping from one company to another without succeeding in any of them. A thief is a metaphor for instant gratification. They want good things without putting the effort, and taking to correct measures towards the goal. These kinds of people view success as a destination, forgetting the process.

The time to start is now. We often say I will think about it. That because we are hoping for the perfect time. I believe that you must get started to make the time perfect. Les Brown "The graveyard is the richest place on earth, because it is here that you will find all the hopes and dreams that were never fulfilled, the books that were never written, the songs that were never sung, the inventions that were never shared, the cures that were never discovered, all because someone was too afraid to take that first step, keep with the problem, or determined to carry their dream." People procrastinate till death. I say to you that now you have heard about the idea of network marketing and Aim Global has proven itself to be the fastest growing company the world, take the opportunity now. Go back to the person who has introduced you to the business and get started. You will also find yourself in the path of givers not takers. I like this quote that say "whoever has will be given more, and they will have an abundance. Whoever

does not have, even what they have will be taken from them" an average person struggle to grasp the message. He that has the right attitude towards life, the desire to succeed, he that lives life of passion and he that has a dream shall get. Only those who are hopeless will suffer and even the little that they have will be taken away and that is your happiness. When you are not doing what you were meant to do, you will never be happy.
Attitude is the most important aspect to success in any venture.

You need three things to be able to successfully court a woman half way around the world: Personal resources, a plan, and commitment. Of these three, commitment is the most important.

If you have commitment, you will find the personal resources and you will persist until you succeed.

We all have the potential within us to achieve great things with our lives. We can be anything we want to be. I think most people would accept the findings of brain researchers that we only use a small fraction of the potential power of our minds.

Most people would accept that if we are prepared to set goals, make plans, and work hard, we are likely to achieve much more with our lives. We would have the ability to build better lives for ourselves and our families, than we would if we just do the minimum required to get by. We may know and accept these things, but that doesn't mean that we are prepared to act on this information and actually do something about it. Why is that? I think that the alternatives are often just too attractive and easy to pursue than to put in the work necessary to achieve our goals.

It may not be that difficult to put in the extra effort required that could make a big difference in our lives, but the reality is that it's much easier not go the easier softer way. There is one overriding factor that makes the difference and determines our actions, and that is our attitude.

Our attitude is the deciding factor to what we experience in life and the attainment of our goals in so many areas of our life.

If your attitude toward your job is that you aren't prepared to do anything outside your job description, or even less if possible, you may feel pleased by getting one over on the boss, but you're unlikely to be considered for a promotion.

Your attitude determines your altitude

Many people enter into a personal relationship with the attitude that because they've been hurt in the past, they are likely to be hurt again. It's this attitude more than anything else that will insure that these predictions are likely to come true.

If you approach problems with a "why does this always happen to me" attitude (a victim mentality), you're likely to not only attract problems, but also have difficulty dealing with them.

Your attitude largely determines your expectations for the future, what you want from your life, and what you are prepared to do to insure you achieve your goals in life. If your attitude is 'what's the point?' or 'it's not worth the effort' you're sure to be proven right.

By the opposite also holds true. If you're prepared to make more of an effort in your job, it's likely that this will be noticed and you will attract promotion and growth opportunities.

If your attitude is generally optimistic and you don't expect to experience problems, you're not only less likely to do so, but when you do, you'll most likely find solutions more easily so you can quickly get back on track.

If you have a positive attitude and look forward to every day for the opportunities it will bring, you will find more opportunities. If you write down your goals, you will make the plans necessary to achieve your goals and take appropriate action. You are well on your way to achieving your ideal life.

With an attitude of positive expectation, you'll not only achieve more, but you'll also experience more satisfaction in your daily life.

Other people can influence our attitudes. The media, our choice of friends, and relatives. We are also affected by our life experiences. Unfortunately, it often seems there are more negative than positive influences.

We cannot control other people or events, and things will happen that we don't like that may affect us in some way. But what we can and must control is how we react to these things. No person or event can control or change our attitude - unless we allow it.

Likewise, no one else can really cause us to become upset or angry. When this happens, we are giving other people control over our lives and relinquishing control of our most basic human right - the control of our own mind. I'm sure you've all seen those signs in offices that go something like 'Everyone brings joy to this office, some when they enter, and some when they leave.'

Which one of these people would you like to be known as? Would you like to be known as a person whose attitude gives the impression they are walking around with a permanent rain cloud over their head. Or would you rather been known as a someone people look forward to seeing? Which person do you think has a happier and more fulfilling life?

A wise man once said, something like 'it's not your aptitude, but your attitude, that determines your altitude.' If your attitude is not working for you, it's probably working against you. Your attitude can be holding you back in ways you don't even realize. No one else can control your attitude; it's all up to you. Change your attitude and change your life.

How to use your story to win prospects?

Once we become members of a networking company, the first people we think of recruiting are our family members. Too often they don't join the business. We then go to our friends and still they don't join the business. This causes frustrations and disbelief. A security company in south African that struggled to find clients, for twenty years of their existence they could only sign up 30 thousand customers. Until one of their partners decided to take the business to the people and knock door to door and in one week they company signed 28 thousand customers. Strangers will often take your business idea seriously if you present it well and you show enough knowledge about the company. So, what will make you stand out in aim global? Go out there and start talking to people, get rejected and move on. Out of 10 at least one will join your team. I have noticed that group presentations are not always as effective than one on one presentations. In a group of 20 people, one person can rub off his negative energy to others.

But when you approach them alone and engage them individual, the likelihood of them join is high.

One of the most important tool when selling a product, it could be C24, Choleduz etc you must be able to tell the story that will connect the customers to the products. When you are pitching the business idea to the next person, you must give them chance to know you by telling a story perhaps what led you to joining the company? Why did you choose this one amongst others? Your ability to tell your story will influence your success in your business.

As networkers we encourage others to dream. We encourage them to live a life of purpose, and we tell them to write it down. We want to see our business partners grow, thus we give them enough support. We are always there to guide them through the business. Sometime, they don't want it enough as we do, so do we quit on them? Or perhaps we have more patience. Selling the dream to them is one thing, but teaching them the skills necessarily for network marketing is another. At times we get caught up in trying to sell them the dream. We tell them joys of network marketing and the amount of money up for grabs, but forgetting that to get to the stage of earning is not as easy as it seems. We need to be examples to our new partners. We should always maintain a sense of integrity. In a way that we treat them with respect even when they are not there. After all, life is the best teacher. I believe we should allow ourselves to fail to succeed. For me networking is a lifestyle more than a business. We cannot talk about health when we ourselves look unhealthy, tell someone to dream big whereas you are filling your body with alcohol and drugs. We must practice what we preach and live what we believe. I met a guy in Dubai who tried to convince me to buy bitcoins. He kept on telling me that the money we are using now will soon be obsolete. His strategy was putting fear in me than listening to my needs. Little did he know that I am a student of financial freedom. Les brown says that as entrepreneurs we got to be strategic and experiential with our stories. That as you pitch your business model, what you are doing is you are distracting, disputing and inspiring. People already have a mind about what it is that they want. When you tell your story about your product, your business, you are disrupting a story that's already their head. So what you want to do is to interrupt that story with you story. Through your presentation you dismantle their belief system and begin to encourage them in the process of your presentation, you create a thirst for what it is that you do. There's a saying that you can take a horse to the water and you cannot force it to drink, however strategically and experientially, you will begin to not only expand their mind the possibilities about what it is that you provide, but you create a thirst for what it is that you provide.

You want to tell your story with confidence. When you speak, you should show confidence and competence about what it is that you are speaking on.

This is one of the uplifting stories I would like to share with you:

How MLM Changed One Girl's Life, by Nancy On (San Jose, California, USA)

The Unexpected Entrepreneur

'I was definitely an "unexpected entrepreneur." Before, I was everything that an entrepreneur was NOT. You wouldn't imagine someone like me would ever be doing business, or anything that involved so much interaction with people!

I was way too reserved, private, and quiet in terms of the standards of entrepreneurship; my network was small and tight. People often wonder how my network marketing organization began to grow so big.

I was 20, almost 21, years old when I was introduced to network marketing. Prior to it, I was a student attending a community

college, and held three jobs to keep myself busy. I really didn't have much passion in school, nor any field that was available. I was living life; doing things that didn't feel purposeful, and didn't make me happy. I just didn't think there was any other way, and I didn't have any true goals that would bring me true fulfilment. I was pretty depressed imagining my future, which consisted of getting stuck in traffic every morning going to my nine to five.'
"I only joined to help my friend" 'I guess one day the person above heard my prayers. My old friend from middle school called me and invited me to a presentation to check out a business with which she just got involved. I really didn't think too much of it, but I said, "Okay, I'll go." I was hesitant because I was never interested in business, nor was I interested in networking with people. Back then, I was extremely quiet and private. I never liked to socialize much, and I kept to a very small circle of friends. It always surprises me how I ended up in this field and became successful at it.

I joined the business mainly to support my friend. I didn't want to say no and turn her down. I didn't think that I would do well at it, so I basically told her, "I'm only doing this to support you; I don't plan to really go full force in it." How ironic! After a few trainings, I saw that this could really change my life, and the system was quite simple to grasp. I saw the bigger picture after realizing the possibility that this could be what I'd always been seeking. Finally, I found an environment that didn't judge me for my past. It gave me a clean slate to earn as much as I wanted without being capped. Finally, I could do something without sitting in traffic every morning, and I could grow this thing as big as I wanted.'

It's not about the money

'Network Marketing has changed EVERY aspect of my life! Being that I am in the health and wellness business, it first and foremost changed my HEALTH. I was a very sickly child. My company's products have dramatically changed my health for the better. Secondly, it gave me a place to build my confidence because I worked in a very encouraging team environment. I had mentors who helped me and pushed me to do things I never thought I could do.

After that, my team continued to grow because I was growing as a person. My income from network marketing has given me the ability to take care of myself and live on my own since the age of 22. At 23, I was able to buy myself the car I've always wanted. And over the years, I have been able to travel to more than 13 different countries. I recently came back from spending two weeks on the island of Santorini, in Greece, as a spiritual gift to myself. Life has been so good to me. I cannot complain, and I am so happy that I get to share what I do for a living with others who want to do the same. I get to wake up when the sun comes up, and I live with a true sense of purpose.

Experiencing Life Through Travel

'One of the most amazing things I've been able to do because of the financial stability in network marketing was travel. I've learned so much about myself and the world by being in different places and meeting new people. It really makes you feel small, and puts everything into perspective. After every trip, I always come back a little different. From hanging out in the Darling Harbor of Australia, to zip-lining in the jungles of Puerto Rico, cave tubing to Belize, enjoying the view on a catamaran in Hawaii, to learning art history in Rome, to meeting such friendly people in Canada, and being fascinated with the culture in Mexico, it's all amazing. I've still got to say that…

One of my most memorable trips was to be able to go to Greece for two weeks by myself. All of my trips before that had been with other people, and they were definitely fun-filled and action packed. However, I decided that I wanted to do something random and outside of my comfort zone.

Traveling solo during an offseason where tourists were not around, was something I will never forget. It felt like I had the entire island to myself. I got to meet the locals and learn the history of Greece from the Greek natives. Most importantly, I discovered things about myself that I never even knew. It felt so good to know that my business had allowed me the ability to pack my bags and fly anywhere in the world at the drop of a dime, even at such a young age. That sense of freedom is unmatched in any career field.'

My Secret Tip to Success

'I'll tell you a secret. It's not all about you; it's about helping and training your people and tapping into their networks. Once I understood the concept that I didn't have to be the best, and I could leverage off people who were better than me, my business took off. I loved the idea that all I needed to do was to be a good supporter of my people and to learn from others who had done it before me. This business is really ingenious if you take time to understand its concept.'

Overcoming doubts from family

'Personally, becoming successful in Network Marketing was very difficult for my parents to grasp. They did not support me at all in the beginning. But when I kept moving forward, their doubts eventually subsided. It repaired the relationship that I had with them. That would have not been possible had I taken another route, one about which I wasn't passionate. I am a passion-driven person. I wouldn't have succeeded in any other field because I just didn't love it. Proving to my family that I found the right path for me here, gave the reassurance they needed. They are now consumers of the product, as well as super supportive of me. Richard Branson is one of my favourite people. He said, "Having a personality of caring about people is important. You can't be a good leader unless you generally like people. That is how you bring out the best in them." Leadership is so important when you are building an organization from scratch. But the coolest thing is that leadership can be learned. After you practice things that leaders do, eventually it will be a habit, and after a while, it will come much more naturally.

Self development is the thing that got me to where I am. There is no possible way that I could have remained the old Nancy and become successful. The old me didn't understand how to be a magnetic person. I didn't understand that building relationships is one of the biggest factors in building a business, or becoming successful in every area of life. Once I understood that, I worked at it day-in and day-out to get better. And the better I got, the bigger my team grew.

This could be you one day. It all starts with a choice. Do ask how, just get started the how will solve itself. There's an old saying 'where there's a will there's a way. We generally make lots of promises to our self-everyday such as to maintain daily routine, daily exercise, finish home work on time, house cleaning, obey parents and teachers, commitment towards study daily, etc. However, sometimes we do not win because of the lack of will power and strong determination. Whenever we see towards our history, we find many great personalities like Nelson Mandela Albert Einstein, Mahatma Gandhi, Edmund Hillary; etc who saw various big dreams and the most important point is that they were able to fulfil their dreams just because they had strong will power towards their goal. They were very clear about their decisions and each step decided for reaching towards the goal.

They never gave up in front of their hard times and continued walking on their way by overcoming all the difficulties. They were able to find out the right path of success. Now-a-days, most of the people of this generation don't have patience and will. Thus, they lack achieving their goal due to their wrong attitudes and greediness. Just think, what will happen if clouds stop raining, sun stop giving sunlight, rivers stop giving water, trees stop giving fruits, etc. We cannot live our life happily if nature stops helping us. We can learn about how to develop commitment towards our work from each and every natural cycle.

This English proverb 'where there is a will there is a way' is means that we cannot succeed in life without having the will power and determination towards the goal achievement. Suppose that a student want to get first position in class without hard work and proper preparation, he/she cannot do the same in any condition as he/she lacks the determination and will of hard work. However, he/she can achieve the goal next year after hard work and complete preparation.

Achieving things which are impossible can be easily obtained by the strong will power and hard work. So, we can possible the things which are impossible through our continuous hard work. We all have internal will power, determination, dedication and capacity of hard work. We just need to recognize our internal strength and develop such natural powers within us to reach to the goal by overcoming all the difficulties of the way. We need to focus on our goal to get ultimate victory because where there is a will, there is a way'.

Here are the benefits of telling a story

- Capture the attention of the prospects or potential investors.
- Motivate individuals and groups to take action
- Build trust and rapport
- Make data and facts sing by becoming applicable, interesting, and relevant
- Infuse information with "stickiness" to improve retention. For example, everyone knows that "slow and steady wins the race."
- Transform beliefs and change minds

These are the entrepreneurs that inspire me daily: Think about how you can use these stories when talking to your prospects.

Milton Hershey.
Milton Hershey had a long path to the top of the chocolate

industry. Hershey dropped out of school in the 4th grade and took an apprenticeship with a printer, only to be fired. He then became an apprentice to a candy-maker in Lancaster, PA. After studying the business for 4 years, Hershey started three unsuccessful candy companies in Philadelphia, Chicago and New York.

Hershey was not about to give up, so he moved back to Lancaster and began the Lancaster Caramel Company. His unique caramel recipe, which he had come across during his earlier travels, was a huge success. Hershey, who was always looking ahead, believed that chocolate products had a much greater future than caramel. He sold the Lancaster Caramel Company for $1 million in 1900 (nearly $25 million in 2008 dollars) and started the Hershey Company, which brought milk chocolate -- previously a Swiss delicacy -- to the masses. Not only did Hershey overcome failure and accomplish his goals, but he also managed to do it close to home. Hershey created hundreds of jobs for Pennsylvanians. He also used some of his money to build houses, churches, and schools, cementing his status as a legend in the Keystone State.

Steve Jobs

The second story is a story of a man we all know, Steve Jobs. He achieved great success at a young age. When he was 20 years old, Jobs started Apple in his parents' garage, and within a decade the company blossomed into a $2 billion empire. However, at age 30, Apple's Board of Directors decided to take the business in a different direction, and Jobs was fired from the company he created. Jobs found himself unemployed, but treated it as a freedom rather than a curse. In fact, he later said that getting fired from Apple was the best thing to ever happen to him, because it allowed him to think more creatively and re-experience the joys of starting a company.

Jobs went on to found NeXT, a software company, and Pixar, the company that produces animated movies such as *Finding Nemo*. NeXT was subsequently purchased by Apple. Not only did Jobs go back to his former company, but he helped launch Apple's current resurgence in popularity. Jobs claims that his career success and his strong relationship with his family are both results of his termination from Apple.

Simon Cowell

Nowadays, Simon Cowell is a pop icon and a very wealthy man. But early in life, Cowell faced his fair share of struggles. At age 15, Cowell dropped out of school and bounced around jobs. He eventually landed a job in the mail room of EMI Music Publishing. Cowell worked his way up to the A&R department, and then went on to form his own publishing company, E&S Music.

Unfortunately, E&S folded in its first year. Cowell ended up with a lot of debt, and was forced to move back in with his parents. But he never gave up on his dream of working in the music industry, and eventually landed a job with a small company called Fanfare Records. He worked there for 8 years and helped the company become a very successful label. From there, Cowell spent years signing talent and working behind-the-scenes before launching the "American Idol" and "X-Factor" franchises that made him famous.

Even though he is rich and successful, Cowell continues to work on new projects. This kind of dedication no doubt helped him overcome his early roadblocks.

Thomas Edison

When he was a young boy, Thomas Edison's parents pulled him out of school after teachers called him "stupid" and "unteachable." Edison spent his teenage years working and being fired from various jobs, culminating in his termination from a telegraph company at age 21. Despite these setbacks, Edison never deterred from his true passion, inventing. Throughout his career, Edison obtained 1,093 patents. And while many of these inventions -- such as the light bulb, stock printer, phonograph and alkaline battery -- were ground-breaking, even more of them were unsuccessful. Edison is famous for saying that genius is "1% inspiration and 99% perspiration."

One of Edison's greatest stories of perseverance occurred after he was already wildly successful. After inventing the light bulb, Edison began a quest to find an inexpensive light bulb filament. At the time, ore was mined in the Midwest, and shipping costs were incredibly high. To combat this, Edison opened his own ore-mining plant in Ogdensburg, New Jersey. For roughly a decade, Edison devoted all his time and money to the plant. He also obtained 47 patents for inventions designed to make the plant run more smoothly. And after all of that, Edison's project still failed thanks to the low-quality ore on the East Coast. But as it turned out, one of the aforementioned 47 inventions (a newly-designed crushing machine) revolutionized the cement industry and earned Edison back nearly all of the money he lost. In addition, Henry Ford would later credit Edison's Ogdensburg project as the main inspiration for his Model T Ford assembly line, and many believe that Edison paved the way for modern-day industrial laboratories. Edison's foray into ore-mining proves that dedication and commitment can pay off even in a losing venture.

George Steinbrenner

Before "The Boss" assumed ownership of the New York Yankees, he owned a basketball franchise called the Cleveland Pipers. The Pipers were part of the American Basketball League, and in 1960, under Steinbrenner's helm, the franchise went bankrupt.

When he eventually took over the Yankees, Steinbrenner's struggles didn't end. Most baseball fans will remember the team's drought in the 1980s and early 1990s. As the team suffered, Steinbrenner was often criticized for his executive decisions, which included questionable trades and frequent changes to the Manager position. Though his methods were controversial, Steinbrenner stuck to his guns, and it paid off. The Yankees made an impressive six World Series appearances from 1996-2003, and remain Major League Baseball's most profitable team year after year.

Steinbrenner is known for his shrewd business tactics, but he's also not afraid to put his money where his mouth is. The Yankees have the highest payroll in baseball, and they've been in contention every year since the mid-90s. Even when the Cleveland Pipers went bankrupt, Steinbrenner offered to pay back the team's investors, a promise he eventually made good on.

Steinbrenner has been quoted as saying, "I never wanted anybody to say 'I went down a path with George Steinbrenner and lost money.'"

J.K. Rowling

J.K. Rowling, author of the *Harry Potter* books, is currently the second-richest female entertainer on the planet, behind Oprah. However, when Rowling wrote the first *Harry Potter* book in 1995, it was rejected by twelve different publishers. Even Bloomsbury, the small publishing house that finally purchased Rowling's manuscript, told the author to "get a day job."

At the time when Rowling was writing the original *Harry Potter* book, her life was a self-described mess. She was going through a divorce and living in a tiny flat with her daughter. Rowling was surviving on government subsidies, and her mother had just passed away from multiple sclerosis. J.K. turned these negatives into a positive by devoting most of her free time to the *Harry Potter* series. She also drew from her bad personal experiences when writing. The result is a brand name currently worth nearly $15 billion.

Walt Disney

As a young man, *Walt Disney* was fired from the Kansas City Star Newspaper because his boss thought he lacked creativity. He went

on to form an animation company called Laugh-O-Gram Films in 1921. Using his natural salesmanship abilities, Disney was able to raise $15,000 for the company ($181,000 in 2008 dollars). However, he made a deal with a New York distributor, and when the distributor went out of business, Disney was forced to shut Laugh-O-Gram down. He could barely pay his rent and even resorted to eating dog food. Broke but not defeated, Disney spent his last few dollars on a train ticket to
Hollywood. Unfortunately, troubles were not over. In 1926, Disney created a cartoon character named Oswald the Rabbit. When he attempted to negotiate a better deal with Universal Studios -- the cartoon's distributor -- Disney discovered that Universal had secretly patented the Oswald character. Universal then hired Disney's artists away from him, and continued the cartoon without Disney's input (and without paying him).

As if that wasn't enough, Disney also struggled to release some of his now-classic films. He was told Mickey Mouse would fail because the mouse would "terrify women." Distributors rejected *The Three Little Pigs*, saying it needed more characters. *Pinocchio* was shut down during production and Disney had to rewrite the entire storyline. Other films, like *Bambi*, *Pollyanna* and *Fantasia*, were misunderstood by audiences at the time of their release, only to become favorites later on.

Disney's greatest example of perseverance occurred when he tried to make the book *Mary Poppins* into a film. In 1944, at the suggestion of his daughter, Disney decided to adapt the Pamela Travers novel into a screenplay. However, Travers had absolutely no interest in selling *Mary Poppins* to Hollywood. To win her over, Disney visited Travers at her England home repeatedly for the next 16 years. After more than a decade-and-a-half of persuasion, Travers was overcome by Disney's charm and vision for the film, and finally gave him permission to bring *Mary Poppins* to the big screen. The result is a timeless classic.

In a fitting twist of fate, The Disney Company went on to purchase ABC in 1996. At the time, ABC was owner of the Kansas City Star, meaning the newspaper that once fired Disney had become part of the empire he created. And all thanks to his creativity (and a lot of perseverance).

As you strategically tell your story, its important to know what to say and when to say it. Look at the type of stories below;

Vision Stories – Communicate your vision and inspire others to act. For example, you could relay a story about how a product or service saved a company. Or, perhaps a company folded because decision-makers didn't act quickly enough.

Who Am I Stories – Demonstrate who you are to people and create that crucial connection. Customers will know you're the type that goes above and beyond when they hear how you saved those kittens from a burning building.

Why Am I Here – Inform customer of your intentions up front and create trust. There's much to be said for being transparent. Customers might become *more* receptive if you tell them what you're trying to sell.

Company Stories – Share knowledge and inform others. To be effective these stories need a "wow" moment. You essentially need to teach listeners something they've never heard or considered. In the context of a story, they'll remember this forever. As a result, they'll remember you and your company forever as well.

My mentor likes saying that if he can do it, you can do it. As Les Brown puts it that we were all born the same, naked and stupid. We can learn. Nothing can stop the will of the people. In South African, for years and years indigenous people were oppressed, they fought for their freedom and were freed. Today people of colour can dream and aspire to succeed because to the will.

Invest in yourself and reinvest in your business

Billionaire investor Warren Buffett says the very best investment you can make is one that "you can't beat," can't be taxed and not even inflation can take away from you.
"Ultimately, there's one investment that supersedes all others: Invest in yourself," Buffett says in a recent interview with Forbes. "Nobody can take away what you've got in yourself, and everybody has potential they haven't used yet." People don't mind paying R300 for a concert, but they find it hard to pay the same amount to buy a book or attend a seminar that will benefit them. I have spoken a number of people about Aim Global and their question is how much do I need to get started. I had a presentation in Malaysia of crew of 4000 people. I believe if it was entertainment people would have come in numbers.
Why is imperative to reinvest In your business. I'm sure you've heard of the phrase "you got to spend money to make money," right? Though it may seem like a cliché saying, it's

actually true. You really do need to spend money to make more money.

Each time we've invested in our own business, we've reaped the rewards tenfold. Whether you're investing in products to help run your business more smoothly, hiring a business coach, or outsourcing tasks, spending the money is worth it. You can't expect to be able to do it all yourself and there are programs and services out there that can save you time (and stress!) on tasks that you don't need to do.

Matt Lloyd says in his article that as your own leads start to convert and you see money coming in, think carefully about what to do with that money. I strongly advise you to reinvest at least half of your profits into the business so that you'll see even larger profits in the future.

Business coach Rasheed Ogunlaru says: "Investment isn't just about cash: Investment is also about time, effort and expertise. It's important to be incredibly resourceful as an entrepreneur."

With that in mind, consider reinvesting in your own training, in hiring skilled employees, or in new traffic avenues. Your primary reinvestments should go to those processes that

Invest in yourself and reinvest in your business

earned profits in the first place! After that, you can get creative and try out new ideas to see how they work.

Aim global offers free trainings to its distributors. It is pro-distributor. This simply means they put distributors before profit. Richard Brandson "clients do not come first. Employees come first. If you take care of your employees, they will take care of the clients." The employees in this case would be the distributors. Aim global offers trainings both online and offline. Their products speak for themselves hence most distributors find it easy to succeed in retailing and recruiting.

What I learned from Robert Kiyosaki

Robert Kiyosaki. Best known as the author of Rich Dad Poor Dad—the #1 personal finance book of all time—*Robert Kiyosaki* has challenged and changed the way tens of millions of people around the world think about money.

The first lesson I learned was that when you give you shall receive The most assured way to receive something is to give. It comes down to your attitude towards money. To make a lot of money requires you give a lot. Not only money, but your time and diligence in working for it. At times there are people who want more, but aren't giving anything.

According to Kiyosaki, your primary aim is to create more value for your customers through your business. You create an excellent product or give exceptional service to your customers so that in return, they will buy more and become your loyal customers. Unfortunately, most people only think about themselves and how they can make the most of their customers. They want to create the cheapest product and wish to get the most from their customers. This will not work out in the long run.

Hence, aim to be a giver. Learn to create more value and how to solve other people's problems. Kiyosaki said that whether you are rich or you are poor, it all lies in your attitude towards money. He said he made a lot of money, but he also gives a lot of money back to the world. Just like what Anne Frank said, "No one has ever become poor by giving."

Is it possible to work less and get paid more? If you want to get paid more, work more! Give more!

Change The Way You Think

Use your challenges as inspiration! Yes, there will be ups and downs. Plenty of the top Entrepreneurs in the world have been in debt. This is where your way of thinking needs to change, to take action and to work hard. Robert Kiyosaki used his problems as motivation to go out and make more money!

'You are your biggest asset and liability.'

How you think will ultimately determine how you live, and like all other successful people, Kiyosaki believes that how we think will determine the results we get in our lives too. He told his story on the Oprah Winfrey Show that like all other business people, he was broke before he became successful. When the bill collectors called, instead of letting those events shrink him and lived in fear, he used them as a motivator to work harder and to pay himself first.

Most people believe that adversity will take them down and block them from going further, but Kiyosaki said that he would think differently and used the adversity as his stepping stone to higher success. Therefore, if you are not living the life you want right now, the first thing you need to do is to change the way you think. When your thinking changed, you will make a different decision and act differently. And eventually, your life will change.

Brian Tracy also said that you will become what you think about most of the time. Highly successful people look at their lives and think differently. Instead of looking at things as a problem, they look at them as an opportunity to learn and grow. And this is how you should think too.

Kiyosaki said that your biggest asset is you. And how you think is the most important key to changing your life. This is why he constantly emphasizes that if someone wanted to get rid of the rat race and become rich, he must change his thinking and learn to be financially educated.

Focus On What WILL Work

Follow One Course Until Successful

Quit trying to do multiple things at once and focus on the project at hand! You can clutter yourself with an overload of things and it can not only be distracting, but also exhausting.

Invest your time into something you know. There is nothing wrong with diversity, but when it slows you down and gets in the way of more important things, then you need to rethink your priorities.

Find what will work for you and stick with it. Each person is different.

In one of his seminars, Kiyosaki shared his view on focus. He said that focus simply means "Follow One Course Until Successful". And that is exactly what he did when he first started. He also said he joined a real estate investment seminar in 1997 and he followed what he has learned from that seminar until he became a master before he decided to become an entrepreneur.

The problem with most people is that they do not have the focus to stay on the course. Most people set goals, attend seminars and learn how to be successful in whatever they do, be it in business or in investment, but they do not follow through. A lot of people want to lose weight and they set it as a goal to hit the gym, to exercise and to eat healthy food. However, only those who stick to the plan are able to achieve the goals.

It is the same in every area of your life. If you want to get rich and be financially free, you must do what Kiyosaki suggested and stayed focus on your course until you achieve the result you desire.

Stop jumping from one opportunity to the next or changing from one business to another business. If you want to be successful, you must stick to your plan, pour in the effort and give it enough time for the result to come.

When you plant a tree, you need to put in the effort to water it, make sure it has enough sunlight and the soil is suitable. However, the tree will not grow immediately the next day. You must give it enough time to sprout and to grow. What most people will do in this case is that they will give up and move on to grow another tree. And when they face the same situation, they will quit and move on to another tree again.

Never let this happen to you. Stay focused and follow one course until you are successful before you switch to another plan.

From Bad Times To New Opportunities

People fall into a negative spin of emotions when economies crash, like when the great depression happened and when the world financial crisis hit quite a few years ago. But some see this as an opportunity to advance.

While some people are worrying, others are using this as an advantage to buy, or resolve the issues, knowing that there is a solution.

Kiyosaki admitted that he made more money when the economy is tough. This is because he believed that the window of opportunity will open when things are tough and everyone looks at it as a dire situation.

When things are tough, people will be in a panic mode and wanted to sell everything, including good businesses that are making a lot of money. Kiyosaki said that he bought five golf courses during the economic downturn because people wanted to sell quickly and they are selling it way below the market price. And he bought them. And a couple of years later, when the economy turns good, he receives great offers to buy the golf courses and this is what makes it a great deal.

The famous author of Think and Grow Rich, Napoleon Hill once said, "Every adversity, every failure, every heartache carries with it the seed of an equal or greater benefit." Highly successful people believe that failures, tough times, adversities, and setbacks are great ways to learn and they contain opportunities to earn and grow higher.

Kiyosaki says that economy is a cycle, it will go up and it will go down. When things are good, the economy will be strong and perform better. When things are tough, the economy will go down and opportunities will be everywhere. And this is why he stresses that financial education is important. You want to learn how to spot the opportunity and make a great deal especially during tough times where the opportunities are everywhere.

Don't be afraid to lose

Every successful people fail at least once in their lifetime. Henry Ford went broke five times before he finally became successful in his automobile business. Steve Jobs, the founder of Apple was fired from the board of directors and the company he started, but he eventually made it back to Apple and built it into one of the most innovative companies of the decade.

And Robert Kiyosaki said that he has failed many times in his businesses too. He also mentioned that his friend, Donald Trump who has co-authored a few books with him also failed many times and was billion-dollar in debt before he bounced back and became even more successful. So, do not be afraid to lose. Kiyosaki shared that babies learn to walk by standing up, falling, and then stand up, and fall again. It is during the falls that the baby learns the most. And it is the same in life and in business.

However, the society and school have conditioned people to believe that failing is bad. When you make a mistake, your teacher will punish you, but you will never punish a baby who falls when she learns to walk, right?

This is the problem with the majority. They are afraid to make mistakes and as a result, they let their fear of failure to stop them from moving forward. So from now on, treat your failure as your feedback to improve yourself and in what you do. *Michael Jordan*, the basketball superstar is famous for his failure quote, saying, "I've missed more than 9000 shots in my career. I've lost almost 300 games. 26 times, I've been trusted to take the game-winning shot and missed."

Be financially educated

Kiyosaki shared a lot of his ideas and concepts on the subject of personal finance. He is an advocate and believes that if someone wanted to be financially successful, he must first equip himself with the necessary financial education.

One of his principles that can change your financial status is to understand what you are working on. In his books, he categorized jobs and careers into four main categories, and they are the employee, the self-employed, the businessman, and the investor.

And you need to understand which category you are in if you want to become rich.

According to Kiyosaki, most of the employed people work for earned income that is being taxed the most. And he said that a large part of the earned income will be gone to pay the taxes before it reaches the employee's hand. He also mentioned that there are three types of incomes.

And when it comes to hard work, the general masses only understand and will work hard for earned income, which is the first type of income according to Kiyosaki. The second type of income is the portfolio income where the majority of it comes from capital gains. For example, when you invest in the stock market and you profit from it, you earned the portfolio income. And the third type of income is the passive income.

What truly makes people rich is the passive income. Kiyosaki suggests his audience to learn and build passive income rather than working hard in a job to earn an income and then get to pay the most tax. This is why he believes that financial education is important because if you are working hard for the wrong thing, you may end up putting in a lot of effort, but only to receive a small amount of result.

Build and grow your asserts

One of the most important success lessons everyone should learn from Kiyosaki is to build and grow their assets. Most people have the wrong perception of assets and liabilities. They thought that a house is an asset. When you buy a house, and move in there yourself, your house is not producing any passive income for you. Instead, you have to put in money for your house such as buying furniture and renovating it.

According to Kiyosaki, assets are things that will bring you money. Things will be different when you buy a property for investment. When you rent out the property, the tenant will be paying you the rental and the rent is a form of passive income. Another great example is your car. A lot of people thought that owning a car is an asset, which is really not. Your car will never bring in passive income for you, and thus, Kiyosaki considers a car as a liability and not an asset.

Therefore, learn to build and grow your assets. Acquire things that will generate you more money rather than take your money away. A well-designed business always increases the number of its assets. And this is exactly what you must do. Aim to acquire more assets that will generate you passive income.

Saving money is obsolete

When it comes to becoming financially successful, what most people will do is to save money. Kiyosaki said that this is not a wise move because you simply cannot keep up with the fluctuations in the value of the currency, which will weaken their buying power. The inflation rate will be higher than the interest you receive from saving money in the bank.

Prices for most things will increase due to inflation. Take oil as an example. In 1997, the oil price per barrel was probably around $10, but after a decade, the oil price has increased to over a hundred dollar per barrel. This is the effect of inflation. And this means that your purchasing power will be greatly decreased as the days go by. And when you saved money in the bank, you are actually losing.

What Kiyosaki suggested is hedging money. Instead of saving all your money, you must hedge it against inflation. When you buy real estate, you are hedging against inflation because when the value of money goes down, the prices for construction materials will go up, and as a result, property prices will go up too. Another good suggestion from Kiyosaki is to invest in gold and silver rather than saving all your hard-earned money in the bank.

The rich don't work for money

Another popular concept from Kiyosaki's book, Rich Dad Poor Dad is that the rich do not work for money, rather, they use their money to work for them. Robert Kiyosaki often says, "Money works for me", and not the other way around.

When you ask people why they are doing all the work, they will tell you that they are working for the money. Most people spend most of their time working to earn a living and to pay the bills. The downside of this approach is that you are exchanging your time for money. And in order to make more money, you will have to sell more of your time working harder and longer hours.

On the other hand, rich and successful people do not work for money. Instead, they build businesses and they make investments so that they receive passive income with little or no work. Rather than spending their time working for money, the rich make full use of their money to work for them.

However, do not misunderstand by thinking that rich people do not work. According to Robert Kiyosaki, rich people just work differently than most ordinary people. They work to acquire more assets that provide them passive income. And this is what you must do too if you want to be financially independent.

Therefore, set goals and work hard to acquire more and more assets. Stop selling your time for money because you only have 24 hours a day. This is why you must think of a way to make your money work for you.

Design Your Business Properly

It's not about the product, it's about designing the business properly without having to raise the capital.

What did you learn from Robert Kiyosaki?
_____
_____
_____
_____
_____
_____
_____
_____
_____
_____
_____
_____
_____
_____

What I learned from Robert Kiyosaki

How to choose a network marketing company and why I chose Aim Global

The Business of the 21st Century

In the 20th Century, we moved in to a new age called the "Industrial Age". The first big corporate giants including Andrew Carnegie and Henry Ford, with their huge steel and car companies dominated the business world. It was whoever owned the factories that controlled the wealth.

From the year 2000 onwards, with the rise of the Internet, we moved in to a new age. "The Information Age".
Today, companies like Twitter and Facebook are changing the business world. Today, it is about building and owning networks. This has levelled the playing field. There has never been a better time in history to build and own your own business. Are you set to take advantage?

Build Your Fortune, Not Someone Else's

Here is the big question: At your current place of work, who is making a living and who is getting rich? It is whoever owns the asset. The asset is the business. This is where the control and wealth is. By working as an "Employee," you are spending your 8-hour day building someone else's asset. You are earning a living, and the owner is building a fortune. You are not only making 10x less money, but also paying twice as much in tax.

Want to Double Your Income Each Year?

It is very difficult to be able to double your income with a job. In fact, the average pay rise is currently around 2%. This is crazy, especially since inflation is closer to 10%. However, with a business, it is a lot easier to get twice as many "customers" next year than the last, which in turn doubles your income. The smart people are now building their own businesses on the side.

True Financial Freedom

One of the top reasons for owning your own business is that it leads to financial freedom. Meaning, being able to earn lots of money without you needing to be there. The problem with a job is that you are "Selling time for money". This means that you can never stop working because your income also stops. With a business, you have hundreds of customers that are generating the income. This means you can go on holiday for a month and be making more money when you come back than when you left.

Utilise the Internet…

Important Point: The Internet is changing the world as we know it, and you are living in the middle of it right now. In 50 years, you might look back and think, why didn't I make the most out of it? There has never been a better time in history to start a business and especially one that involves connecting with people. You can now contact hundreds of people with a push of a button. The fact you are reading this right now proves its effectiveness. You will kick yourself if you do not take advantage of this.

Living A Rich and Rewarding Life

One of the biggest benefits with a network marketing business is the personal development, which many people are not even aware it exists. To become successful, you have to help other people become successful. It's very rewarding to watch other people grow and become better people. The fact that you can make £100K per year, working only 4 hours a day, which then gives you all the time and money to enjoy life is a massive bonus.

Are You Taking Advantage of the Population Boom?

You may not currently be aware of this but, the human race is currently expanding exponentially. Simply do a Google image search for "world population growth" and you will see world population is going off the chart. Now, this is going to cause a lot of problems for some businesses, but is great for people businesses like network marketing.

What Job Security?

For over 100 years, the reason people clung to jobs was because of security. Today, with more and more people getting made redundant in a shrinking market, job security no longer exists. People are now looking for a more secure way to earn a living. What is more secure? Having one income stream with a job or an income coming from a hundred places, which you get from having a customer base? Today, jobs are now the risky option..

Want to Work for The Next 50 Years?

People now have a clear choice. Do they graduate from university with R200K of debt? They can then either get a job, earn a living and retire in 50 years on the equivalent of minimum wage, or, they can build a business and have the opportunity to retire after only 3-5 years. This is the Industrial Age moving in to the Information Age at it's most obvious. Those who realise this, will be the ones who will benefit massively financially.

. Want to Start Life R200K in Debt?

With university fees being tripled in the South Africa, the average student debt is now R200K. The younger generation are starting life with chains around their neck. The choice the younger generation now has, is going to university and starting life in debt or starting a business where in 3 years they could become financially independent. Where do you think people are going to be going? Are you ready to help them and benefit financially?

Do You Use Mass Market Chemical Products?

Did you know that 95% of the food we buy and personal care products we use from the super markets and the high street stores are not very good for you? They are mass produced and in order for them to have a long "Shelf Life" are being pumped full of preservatives and parabens. Studies are now linking these to cancer. The top network marketing companies are botanically based meaning, products that are actually good for you.

. Would You Like an Income That Builds Itself?

When you get to a certain point in a multi level marketing business and you have your team in place, your business then begins to build itself. You cannot do this with a job. This is how you can go then away on holiday and be making more money when you come back than when you left. Thats leverage!

Want More Recognition and Appreciation?

How would you like to work for a company where your hard work gets regular recognition and appreciation? You can now become part of a strong community of people who all want you to succeed as it directly benefits everyone. This is very rare to find in a job.

The 9-5 Job Is Broken!

In a 9-5 job, there is only one winner and that is the boss. The reason you only get 2% pay rises is because it comes directly out of the boss's pocket. The more money you make, the less money he makes. In a mlm business, the more money you make, the more money your business partners make. It is a true win/win. This is not only the business modal of the future, it is the business modal of right now.

Surround Yourself With Like Minded, Fun, Ambitious People

Are you lucky enough to be surrounded by fun, ambitious, like minded people? Most people are not. Network marketing attracts the very best people, which is very beneficial to you because you then surround yourself in a new culture that supports you and helps you become successful. Remember this: You will earn what the 5 closest people around you earn.

A Shrinking Job Market

With increasing population and more traditional businesses closing down due to the Internet, there are now less jobs for people to go for. This means employers can and do take full advantage of this, asking people to work longer and longer hours for the same money. This is becoming more and more common and is making people work in a fear based environment. Do you want to continue to live like this?

Getting Poorer with Rising Prices? – Inflation!

So, the government statistics state that inflation is around 3%…so why then are our gas, electric and phone prices going up closer to 10%? You don't need a degree in maths to know this doesn't add up. The truth is that if you are not getting closer to a 10% pay rise each year, then you are actually getting poorer. Inflation is a stealth tax which the masses are not educated to realise.

Want the Same Tax Breaks of the Rich?

Having a part time or full time home business gives you great tax incentives that are used by the rich. All of a sudden, all your transport, rent, computer, phone, office equipment, coffee shop visits, meals out, as well as many other things all become a tax deductible expense. You too can have access to tax incentives that rich people get to use.

What Do Donald Trump, Richard Brandson and Robert Kiyosaki Have In Common?

I am going to finish with this. Some of the biggest business people all around the world are either involved or recommend network marketing, including Donald Trump, Richard Brandson, Robert Kiyosaki, Stephen Covey, Jim Rohn and T Harv Eker and many more. Who are yo

Why I chose Aim Global?

There are thousands of network marketing companies in the world. The tricky part is choosing the one that resonates with you. I am not going to mention any other company beside the one that transformed my life, and I believe that it could also do the same for you.
Here are some of the questions you should ask yourself before choosing a network marketing company.
Has the Company Been Around for at Least Five Years?
If you want the efforts you put in today to pay off for many years in the future, choose a company that has proven that it will be around for the long term.

Approximately 90 percent of all network marketing companies fail within their first two years. You don't want to invest your precious time and resources—not to mention your future—in something that may not be in business next month.

Is the Company Well-Capitalized?

Does the company have the cash that it will need to grow, to maintain a solid infrastructure, to attract talented management, to keep pace with technology, and to pay your commissions? Does the Company Offer Products or Services That Are Unique? Ensure that the products or services are not readily available elsewhere—especially at a discount—and they're not just another "me too" product or service that has loads of competition.

Is There a Genuine Need for the Product or Service?

You've probably heard horror stories about people ending up with a garage full of expensive water filters or other items. This happens because only other distributors will purchase the product at that price. Your product or service must fill a *real* need at a fair price, and there should be a large untapped market for it. In other words, it must provide tremendous value so that the customer is the biggest winner.

Is the Product or Service Trendy or a Fad?

You can't build long-term residual income if the product or service only has short-term appeal—e.g., beanie babies, etc. Think long term instead. Is the product or service something that your customers will continue to use for a long time?

Can You Generate Immediate Income?

You need to be able to finance your marketing and expansion efforts from cash flow. Having to invest hundreds or thousands of dollars now only to see a return on investment months from now is not a good strategy.

Does the Marketing System Take Full Advantage of Technology?

Not everyone is a sales type, but anybody can plug into a system and tools that do the selling and sorting for you. This can be as simple as scripts or email campaigns or as full-blown as an entire marketing funnel. The important thing is that you're given a marketing system that is already proven to work and not required to trial-and-error your own.

Is the Person Who Is Introducing You to the Opportunity Committed to *Your* Success?

If they are, the company is strong, and the product or service is a winner, you will succeed.

You will have to put the effort in to learn the systems and processes that make it work, but there's a big difference between a sponsor and a recruiter. A sponsor coaches, motivates, and trains and a recruiter just signs people up and, in most cases, abandons them once their commission is collected.

Is There a Way to Build Your Business Part-Time Without Losing Your Full-Time Income?

The company must have automated systems that can do the heavy lifting—selling and sorting—for you so that you can use your limited time efficiently. Being able to build your business part-time while keeping your full-time income is the least risky way to transition to a new source of revenue.

Will You Have Fun?

Although this may not be an element of your current job, it is important. You should have fun with your business partners while you work together to build a long-term business and your financial army.

So there you have it—10 criteria for selecting a superior network marketing opportunity. Of course, even with a great company, there's no such thing as a free lunch. You *will* have to work! However, with the right opportunity, your job won't have to be forever.

Why Aim Global is the right choice?

Well Established – AIM Global is proven and well-established company. Founded on March 2006 and for 10 years in business, AIM GLOBAL never failed to pay the commissions of every distributor EVERYDAY

Quality Products – AIM Global products are world-class and not just an ordinary product. Imported and made by Nature's Way U.S.A. WEIDER of Switzerland, Asia Life Science of Japan and DSM Europe. The products are proven effective at reasonable price. Therefore, the reorders are high because it is food supplements and consumables that can be consume by anyone from pregnancy to bonus age.

Exclusivity of Products – AIM GLOBAL products are exclusive for the company and you cannot buy from your leading stores nationwide.

Innovative – AIM Global NEVER stops to discover new products especially for health, so the product lines are growing from time to time. This year alone (2016) there are new products, Ipro-Tect 24/7 and care a leaf , AND the Nutraceuticals.

Transparent – Because you have online account, you can monitor all activities including your group wherever you are in the world. You can see your commissions, payouts & points every day and nobody can steal it from your account because it is secured with your personal username and password.

Experienced and Trustworthy Owners – AIM GLOBAL owners are directors experienced NETWORKERS, so they know how to distribute the products, explain the products and marketing plan and to operate the company.. Because of these, there is no overpaying. You can see them in the office and sometimes they conduct seminars and trainings. You can talk to them and you can ask them some advice. They care to us and all distributors of the company because they know how to be a distributor.

Global Expansion – AIM GLOBAL is NOT limited only to the Philippines. It is legally spreading to the whole world, and the truth is, AIM GLOBAL already has offices in Singapore, Brunei, Hongkong, Taiwan, Dubai, Hawaii, South Korea, Kuwait,Nigeria,Kenya, Ghana, Togo, Ivory coast, Cameroon,Indonesia,India,and Pakistan There are many other offices that soon to open in other countries like South Africa and other European countries this year. This is the proof that the company is going stronger and they are not afraid to expand globally. Now in 2016, its division is continually expanding to 200 countries and territories around the world.

Top-notch Marketing Plan – The marketing plan of AIM Globalis not only limited to Binary. It is the combinations of Hybrid Binary, UniLevel and Stair Step. So, in just 1 effort, you will earn 3 times. There are many networking companies out there, but only AIM GLOBAL has the combinations of the 3 marketing plans. because of this we are voted as the top 1 compensation plan in the world for 2015 by

Scholarship Program – AIM GLOBAL is giving away scholarship to all members up to 100% discounts on tuition fees which is transferrable to anyone depending to schools and courses. It is a very big help to those who wants to pursue studying in college. How about your company? Did your company give you scholarships?

Alive Foundation – AIM GLOBAL is unique, it is not just an ordinary networking company that cares only for money. They are doing charity works; AIM GLOBAL is helping poor people NATIONWIDE and giving away relief goods to the needy. This is the reason why the company is growing very fast and lots of blessings and abundance.

I would also like to share this incredible testimony of a man who survived cancer, as result of using aim global products. She shared her story in an article that was posted by Marc Bryson / February 6, 2016 :

A STORY OF LOVE AND HOPE THAT ABOUNDS THE GARCIA FAMILY SHARES THEIR MIRACLE

The Garcia couple works at the San Bernardino Hospital: Vicente as a Finance Officer and Emily as a Purchasing Officer. So, when Vicente was diagnosed with *Laryngeal Cancer*, it was a grave concern not only for his family but also for the majority of the hospital officials. They didn't waste any time, chemotherapy was performed right away. And Emily, having to struggle with the expensive treatment and much emotional stress, realized that the story she sees day after day in her workplace had now become her own reality. *"Now, I know how they feel,"* she admitted thinking. Emily and their children saw the pain Vicente had to endure as he underwent radiation. Yet they remained positive because of their unwavering faith and constant prayer for mercy. But two months later, when the CT scan and biopsy results were brought to them by the Oncologist, Emily recalls, *"The way he walked towards us warned us of the coming blow. The doctor said that for Vicente to live, his throat has to be removed and after he gets some rest, he needs to go through another cycle of chemo."*

"That moment still haunts me to this very day", Emily continued. *"My heart sank as I gently caressed my husband's cold hands, our eyes met, and I knew we were thinking the same thing: the end was near. The doctor and I both knew he wouldn't be able to survive eight, or even just one more session of chemo. We prayed together, and with much conviction, placed my husband's life before God."*

The treatment that followed took a huge financial toll on them but she wasn't going to give up on Vicente. She began to research and looked for alternative solutions until a few of her friends shared some articles through Facebook about *AIM Global*. *"I learned that they have a product that gives hope to the hopeless. Through a cousin of mine, a schedule was set and I met with Dr. Lori Dela Cruz."*

"The four months of chemotherapy didn't seem to help him improve. He was bed-ridden and his condition looked really bad. That's when we decided to have him take C24/7, three capsules daily. After three months of intake, we noticed that the supplements have clearly improved his health. So much so that

when he went through another Laryngoscope, by God's miracle, he was cleared of the cancer!

The doctors who witnessed this incredible recovery were so amazed! The Oncologist himself became an AIM Global Distributor!"

Source: AIM HIGH – Official Newsletter of Alliance in Motion Global, Inc. Vol.4 No.1

Keeping your integrity in network marketing

David Whitmore 18, 2015: contents that Network Marketing is a huge business these days. With the wealth of social media sites, such as Facebook, Twitter, Google + and LinkedIn giving us access to thousands of people, it's so simple for us to get our message out there. And then of course there are the blog sites such as WordPress. This is a double-edged sword. On the one hand, it's so easy *anyone* can do it. On the other hand, it's so easy anyone can do it. Even without knowing the best way to go about it.

When a person decides to go into business with you, whether as a customer or as a business builder, it isn't just your business that attracts their attention. No matter how good your business is, what's the first thing your prospective customer is going to see?

You.

You are their first port of call. You are the person behind the company, the person they are going to talk to. You aren't just promoting your business. You're promoting yourself. And as they listen to your sales pitch they are going to be thinking one thing.

Can I trust you?

Trust is the most important element, the glue that holds your business together. It's one of those things that can be so hard to gain. But, so easily lost. As you tell them what you have to offer, you need to be up front and honest. Because if you lie to them, if you make it sound so easy when it's not, they are not going to stay with you once they learn the truth. So, you must prove to that person you are worthy of their trust. To do that, you must be trust*worthy*. Internet marketing isn't just about making money. Obviously, that's the biggest reason we do it. But, it can't be our only focus. If you're looking for customers you must provide a good level of service. It's not just about making a sale. Especially if you want them to come back for more. If you are looking to bring someone into your business to partner with you, then you have to make it all about that person. You need to put their needs first if they are going to stay with you for the long term.

Remember, trust is hard to gain but so easily lost.

We've been active on Facebook a lot the last couple of weeks. We joined a lot of work from home groups. We've seen good practices. And we've seen bad practices. Some people pretend they're looking for a business to work with and ask you to friend them and send them a message with more information. When you do, they pretty much ignore you. But behind your back they're trolling through your friend list, messaging your friends, trying to prospect them. I made a post on Facebook about this. A couple of people tried to make out it wasn't such a bad tactic. But we're not convinced. Most of us use Facebook to keep in touch with our family and friends. Most of our family and friends have no interest in networking. So, we don't feel they should be subjected to messages from people prospecting them. I don't know, maybe we're just naive. We're in a great business with the intention of helping people both with their finances and with their health. Yes, we also want to make money. But not at any cost. Not at the cost of our integrity. We want to be able to look prospective business partners in the eye and let them see that yes, they can trust us. Maybe we won't make as many contacts this way. Maybe we won't make as much money as some of the more bullish networkers. But we'll get there. And we'll have the satisfaction of knowing we did it the right way and we haven't hurt anybody.

Keeping your integrity in network marketing.

People sometimes think that network marketing is all about making a quick money and signing people up without reaching out and caring about who it is they are signing up. No wonder some might say, 'this company or that company is a scam'. I tell people to stop and think about who the company is and the person they are partnering with.

Integrity is always important! YOU are the business. The way YOU do business is what people will see and think about what you do as a whole.

This MUST be a way of life in ALL our dealings with people. As we are in the home and personal life… so we will be in our business life. Customers now days are looking for transparency in the businesses they support. The days of success by hiding behind smoke and mirrors are gone. Social Media has seen to that. Trust begets more word of mouth power and buys more trust.

Keeping your integrity in network marketing.

Write down five reasons why it is important to keep your integrity in network marketing?

Upline and downline relationship

Your upline is the one that introduced the business to you. But he doesn't have much control in your success. The starring in this scene is you. Seb Brantigan (date unknown) postulates : Before I go into this, remember that the upline downline relationship is not the same as a boss employee relationship! If you're the upline, here is what you need to know.

One of the big problems you might face are people wanting to quit your organisation. Some will just leave, and others will likely write a 'Dear Majola letter' upon their exit or potential exit. I wouldn't recommend chasing or begging people to stay, but I am one to give some words of advice to people who are looking to quit.

With that said, I would never discourage someone from changing companies or make them feel guilty for wanting to jump ship. You never know who might come back down the line!

Upline and downline relationship

Things do change over time, so be sure to retain that relationship and don't make your downline feel like you are only friends with them so long as their auto ship is active. Make this the friends for life program and you will have a powerful network over time.

I also recommend giving your downline a lot more value than what they paid for. Do regular trainings to help new people, and work with the people getting the results instead of those who are not putting in the effort!

Go forward with WINNERS in your life and leave the losers behind. This is no time to have unmotivated sad, pitiful energy draining people in your life! You can run faster with 10 motivated people going for a dream than with one toxic person around your neck. Find the courage to cut the ties with anyone who will take you back to a life that is no longer you. Don't take their calls or feel sorry for them. They are a part of your past, so keep it that way. Seek out, find, and maintain new relationships with people who are driven, creative, ambitious, and inspiring to be around...people who will stretch your mind and your life vision. Life is about growing in every dimension of who you are, and manifesting your GREATEST life! You deserve!

I would like to leave you with this poem, yes, you might have read it before, but I want you to ponder on what this book has taught you, then decide whether you are a winner or a loser. Remember losers are not people who fail, but who do not attempt anything at all.

If you want it bad enough

by Les Brown

If you want a thing bad enough to go out and fight for it, to work day and night for it, to give up your time, your peace and sleep for it… if all that you dream and scheme is about it, …and life seems useless and worthless without it… if you gladly sweat for it and fret for it and plan for it and lose all your terror of the opposition for it…if you simply go after that thing that you want with all your capacity, strength and sagacity, faith hope and confidence and stern pertinacity…if neither cold, poverty, famine, nor gout, sickness nor pain, of body and brain, can keep you away from the thing that you want…if dogged and grim you beseech and beset it, with the help of God, YOU WILL GET IT! – Les Brown

Why giving is important?

Alive foundation is a charitable organisation of Aim Global spearheaded by the brilliant, kind-hearted, extraordinary Dr. Connie Malubay-Cabantog. Alliance is motion is more about giving than taking and I'm going to share with you why giving will ALWAYS be more valuable than taking/receiving.

The first reason is appreciation

The world is full of people who only want to help themselves and leave everyone in the dust. Fortunately, the people with that mentality are the ones who get left in the dust. When working with someone who merely treats you like a customer, they are easily distinguishable.

People want to work with others who value and appreciate them, no matter what. People would rather deal with those who see them as a friend and not just a few extra Benjamin Franklins.

Those who care about their customer's health, family, relationships, and career are always going to stand out.

The funny thing about giving information, services, knowledge, and expertise without asking for anything in return, is that when you're beyond helpful, they almost want to throw their money at your face for how much you value helping them.

Believe it or not, business is 100% about giving to the customer; not taking from them.

You might have the best product in the world and there's no denying it, but no matter how good it is, building a relationship and being dedicated to solving their problem will always triumph.

Word Of Mouth.

Now is the time to turn a start-up into a multi-million rand or peso business purely by word of mouth. Giving more than receiving greatly capitalizes on that statement.

We live in a world where news spreads almost instantly. The internet and social media have changed businesses forever. Businesses that are not adapting, focusing on the importance of customer retention, and building a social media brand are going to be forgotten or fail eventually.

When you leave a customer with a bad experience you could lose 3, 4 or even 100 customers. When you leave them with a good experience, that is you potentially gaining 4, 5 or even 50 long-term customers.

Are you starting to understand why giving is more important? It's not always about giving things away, but being of so much value that your competitors are pretty much forgotten.

You can do this by sending follow up letters, asking about family, throwing a couple free items, discounts, or just genuinely exceeding expectations in any way possible.

If you go the extra mile for them, they will go the extra mile for you.

Being unique, understanding, and relatable are things that will 100% separate you from the pack of wolves.

The Good Feeling

For some people, giving puts off a bad feeling. For others, it moves them and fuels their internal drive.

If you're like me, when you give to someone or help someone, it puts a smile on your face and makes you feel special. I'm actually the type of person that feels as if I can accomplish anything after going out of my way to help others. It sounds silly but I truly feel that way.

I think about the millions of people who only care about themselves and would never even toss a quarter to a homeless man or spend a moment of their time helping another person. I can't relate to those people.

I'm grateful to know that giving will get me further in life.

I absolutely love giving money to the homeless. I won't throw out more than I can afford, but giving away a R50 to see someone smile and have their day made is well worth it.

When I give even R50 away to the homeless, it leaves me with this sense of accomplishment that I can do something incredible just by giving.

I despise when I hear the statement regarding giving a homeless money;

"oh, he'll just buy booze" or, "He'll just buy cigarettes".

It might be true; he or she might just buy booze, cigarettes, and maybe even drugs, but it's not about what he does with the money; that is his choice.

Regardless of what he uses the money for, it was my choice to help him and I know it's the right thing to do. I know God will thank me for sparing some money once in a while to help someone struggling 50x more than I am. I don't care what they do with it, It's the fact that I made the right decision.

I want to work extremely hard in life so I can give on a scale I am currently not capable of now. The sense of accomplishment that would come from donating over 100 grand would be like no other feeling. Not everyone feels that way but I can guarantee you those who do will make a much bigger impact on the world.

It's so important to understand that this doesn't mean you shouldn't strive to win and be better than your competition. It means that doing so in a giving, caring, and compassionate way is the game changer. If you want results, you need to be willing to put out 10x the effort of what you hope to receive in return for your hard work.

Being someone who only cares about receiving and taking from individuals may seem like the quicker and smarter path. Those who focus purely on exceeding expectations with clients and customers will always be in first place.

Contributing to a community or organization that aligns with your interests and values can be incredibly rewarding. Instead of serving yourself, you are serving others, and the good feelings that come with that approach are unlike anything you'll experience.

A lot of people stress about finding careers or families that will bring them joy. For me, I always wanted to see how I could contribute to a project that didn't wallow in the routine or the been-there-done-that. And if you catch me smiling randomly, now you know why.

Many thanks to Dr. Ed Cabantoq

Mr. Jonh Aspirin

Engr. Francis Miguel

More power to the Aim Global Family

How to Think and Achieve BIG

The reason why you are reading this book is because you want to change your life. This is ultimately why you invested with Aim Global.

Be Positive & Fearless.
Negative or fearful thoughts produce small thinking. Think positively. Eliminate the word 'impossible'. Successful big thinkers come up with reasons why you 'can'. Others find reasons why you can't. Whichever way you think, it becomes a self-fulfilling prophecy. Big thinkers see problems as a challenge, and any challenge as an opportunity. Their big thinking creates unlimited possibilities, alternatives and solutions. Turn your attention to being brave, bold and optimistic. It is exciting and challenging. Go for it!

Visualise Without Restraint.
It is not a lack of resources that holds people back, but a lack of resourcefulness. A big thinker visualizes what is possible in the future, rather than being stuck in the present. Look at things not

as they are now, but as they can be – without constraints. Visualization adds value to everything. This mental rehearsal gives you a compelling taste of what your vision will be like in reality, and the impetus to make it happen. Come up with creative solutions to realise your goals.

Ask BIG questions.
Practise asking yourself and others some really big and challenging your questions, such as: If there was one thing you could change about the world, what would it be? If you had an unlimited supply of money, what would you do? If you had all the time in the world, what would you do?
Who in the world would benefit the most from what you know?

Feedback from other people discussing such big questions is invaluable. Ask your associates huge questions that open up your thinking about business. Top leaders spend much more time requesting advice than they do giving it – and it's how they put ideas into action that can change the world.

Be Creative and Dream Big.
Go large. The size of your belief determines the size of your success. Do some blue-sky thinking or creative brainstorming

without censorship. Think about how you can develop them into reality. The key to success is imagination, so let your ideas flow freely, allow yourself to dream, take note of your greatest idea then concentrate on that and don't give up until your vision is a reality. Dreams fan the flames of burning desire, high aspirations, and compelling goals in life. Create a vision that is so inspirational that it ignites the fire within you and gets you excited to work towards it.

Set a Massive Long Term Goal and Stick to it.
 Turn your attention to what you want, and make it happen. What you focus on, and what you take action on, you will get. Successful people are those who are doing everything they can to achieve their goals.

Inspire Those Around You.
Successful people connect with people, and confidence attracts others, so use these qualities to bring others onside. The ability to leverage and inspire others is key: the bigger you think, the more people you can get on board. Big ideas motivate and inspire those around you, and in this highly connected world it has never been easier to attract and build a following around a big idea. Through social media, big ideas can spread quickly and gain the resources

they need to make them happen. Leverage those around you to give yourself the best chance of making your ideas a reality.

Take Action & Eat the Elephant One Bite at a Time – Take action. Goals are dreams that are captured, pinned down and action-planned. Followed through by action, they ensure success. Take steps towards your big goal on a daily basis: even spending just 15 minutes per day will help you to achieve great success, over a 10 year period.

Above all: Believe in Yourself.
Belief is the most important part of achieving big. If you believe it can happen, it can happen. Magnify your thinking power. To quote the big thinking and achieving Steve Jobs: "Life can be much broader, once you discover one simple fact, and that is that everything around you that you call life was made up by people that were no smarter than you. And you can change it, you can influence it, you can build your own things that other people can use. Once you learn that, you'll never be the same again." Be confident – know that you can do it, and you will be unstoppable!

Never underestimate the power of your thoughts – and make them big. All inventions start off as big ideas, and big thinkers can

How to think big?

change the world. They are leaders, innovators and achievers because they are free from limitations and small thinking. Thinking big widens your horizons, taking you out of the ordinary and into the extraordinary.

Practise putting this thinking into effect, and take action. Put no limits on your goals. Go for bigger and better, and have the passion, drive and energy to make your dreams into reality. Expand your mind, your thinking, and expand your horizons. Go large! Make it happen.

MORE POWER!

Acknowledgements:

I would like to express my gratitude to the many people who saw me through this book; to all those who provided support, talked things over, read, wrote, offered comments, allowed me to quote their remarks and assisted in the editing, proofreading and design. I would like to thank Amazon for enabling me to publish this book. Above all I want to thank my wife, Susan and the rest of my family, who supported and encouraged me despite all the time it took me away from them. It was a long and difficult journey for them.

I would like to thank Hajah Fauziah for helping me in the process of selection and editing. Thanks to Dr. Aammton who encouraged me.

Last and not least: I beg forgiveness of all those who have been with me over the course of the years and whose names I have failed to mention."

About the author

Moshe Richard Shokane is a business coach, life coach, network marketer and a teacher by profession. He helped several international small businesses thrive in these uncertain economic times.

www.ingramcontent.com/pod-product-compliance
Lightning Source LLC
Chambersburg PA
CBHW031927240526
45464CB00023B/1903